Hunting Ducks and Geese

Hard Facts, Good Bets, and Serious Advice From a Duck Hunter You Can Trust

Steve Smith

Line drawings by David Roebuck

Stackpole Books

Published by
STACKPOLE BOOKS
Cameron and Kelker Streets
P. O. Box 1831
Harrisburg, PA 17105

Cover photograph by Joseph Workosky.

Printed in the U.S.A.

Library of Congress Cataloging in Publication Data

Smith, Steve.
    Hunting ducks and geese.

    1. Waterfowl shooting. I. Title.
SK331.S55 1984   799.2′44   84-2630
ISBN 0-8117-0461-0

For Rich and Jo,
my first teachers who gave me my love of the
outdoors, the wonder to make me ask why,
and in doing so, probably created a monster.

Contents

Acknowledgments

I'd like to take this chance to thank some people who helped make doing this book a little easier.

Thanks go to Jerry Warrington, who took the time to run down some of the data I needed to complete the weather section. I'd also like to thank Charlie Lichon and John Stevens for permission to expose them to the world as known waterfowlers.

I'd like to thank my kids, Amy, Chris and Jake, for understanding why the office door is closed for weeks on end whenever I hole up to write a book. And, I'd be remiss if I didn't mention the artwork of David Roebuck and the photography of Steve Griffin and Joe Workosky.

Finally, thanks to Sue and Amy, who typed the manuscript for me.

Foreword

Peering out through the refuge windows, you note that darkness still reigns supreme over the marsh. The quiet spatter of sleet against the glass is nearly lost amidst the on-going chatter from the morning's participants.

Swallowing the last bit of coffee from the styrofoam cup, you make your way toward a refill, exchanging an occasional "Think they'll be flying?" or "How's your season been?" with men whose faces are all too familiar, yet whose names somehow escape you. Not that it matters, really. The acknowledgments stem from the recognition that they, like you, are here to try their hand at gunning the flights south. Regardless of the outcome and in spite of the weather, your mutual addiction to the sport is the common ground.

Presently, your partner pulls you aside and starts laying out the morning's game plan in hushed tones to avoid being overheard by the other gunners. "Blind number 3 over in the northern corner of the flooded timber has had some good shooting," he whispers, "and so has number 16 just off to the south edge of the river flats." Glancing up, you calculate the kill figures—a feat in itself considering how little sleep came your way—and find yourself nodding in agreement, adding that ol' number 32 might be a good choice as well if the shooting gets heavy on the federal refuge and the birds start looking elsewhere.

And, then the drawing begins. As the refuge personnel begin pulling numbers, the blind assignments are handed out. In complete disregard for past traditions, you draw fourth, choosing number 16 as *your* spot among the markers on the refuge map. Finally, the last number is pulled, and you shuffle out to the car and drive to the nearest point of entry, hoping to shorten the distance you and your gear must travel before reaching the blind.

The engine noise fades at the turn of a key. The silence and darkness become all consuming, except for the glow from your partner's pipe and the sounds of the ever-present sleet and your Lab shuffling nervously in the back seat. You slip into your waders with about as much grace as a circus fat lady trying to wiggle into a size 10 girdle. The struggle culminates with your departure from the front seat into the weather.

Once outside, the distant sound of waking waterfowl filters in through the soft tapping of frozen rain against the brim of your camouflage hat. A smile breaks across your face as you realize the weather isn't going to lift. Reaching back inside, you notice your partner grinning at nothing in particular as he listens to the early-morning chatter. The parka is first to be added, followed by a necklace full of calls, half a box of shells on both sides, and two pair of gloves. Finally, the autoloader is uncased, checked once and then again to be sure it's empty. With that, you shoulder the bag of decoys and the trio cuts a direct line to the blind—you, your partner, and your dog.

Your arrival is marked by the first sliver of eastern light cutting across the sky. Decoys are set, more or less, in acceptable fashion. Then, you hunker down against the wall of your blind, eyes glued to the luminous face of your watch as legal shooting time approaches. As one flight after another makes a run over the blocks, you assure your partner for the 17th time in less than five minutes that your watch was synchronized with the refuge clock just before you left.

At long last, it arrives. With a nod of your head, you give your partner the go-ahead and the calling commences. The first of a long string of mallards pitch into your decoys and you stand and take 'em as they fight for speed and altitude.

So it goes. As the final hours of shooting come to an end, you pack your decoys into the bag, shoulder your birds and your gun, and leave the blind for the winners of the afternoon draw. And, somewhere along the way, you pause for just a moment and silently wish the same sort of luck to those who'll gun the twilight flights.

In effect, such is the life of today's waterfowler. Though his methods and the rules governing his harvest of birds have changed the complexion of the sport, one thing has remained the same— a love of blinds, retrievers, and the birds themselves. Once waterfowling gets into your blood, little can ever take it away. Steve Smith is evidence of that.

Like many of us who still choose to wade the icy waters of November and gun the flights, Steve understands the reasons for steel shot, shorter seasons and the point system. Unlike others, however, he hears the lonely call of a wedge of Canada's finest not as a proclamation of their arrival, but as an announcement of their departure and a promise that someday they will return. In the marshes, he is the best of partners both as participant and as observer, and that is a rare combination.

This book is the best of all worlds. It offers a myriad of tips and hints woven in among some excellent anecdotes, and allows you the pleasure of exceptionally fine reading. In short, it's typical Smitty—enjoyable reading with more than a hint of proof of point.

With that, I leave you in the competent hands of one Steve Smith. Regardless of your years in the marsh, I feel safe in assuming that the following pages will gift you with a smile and perhaps add a new wrinkle or two to your technique. And, best of all, will be the reflections of duck blinds past as the observations of a fellow gunner touch home . . .

Jerry Warrington

1

There and Then

If you're like me, there are times when you wish that you were born about a century ago, born wealthy, and were a waterfowl hunter back when the ducks darkened the sun. I like to imagine what we would be like, you and I, in those never-to-be-seen-again days . . .

We arrive at camp late Friday night after a week of going one-on-one with the other captains of industry in the city. Our financial standing enables us to hold membership in our club, which features more or less plush accommodations, dog-boarding facilities, manservants and a good-natured cook/housekeeper who thinks of us as her "boys."

Friday is spent trying to figure out what they print on the

bottom of Virginia Gentleman bottles, swapping stories of business ventures, of fortunes made and lost, of what the new administration is likely to do, or of Nash Buckingham's newest book.

But, eventually, the talk turns to the next day's gunning. Along about the time that dinner has finally settled a bit, Old Eustus pads into the room where we stand or recline around a fireplace that is big enough to roast an ox in. He makes a few cryptic comments about the wind direction and speed and the chances of rain, suggests what type of gear to wear in the morning, and finally assigns blinds—Mr. Wilson to the Three Ponds, Mr. O'Hara to the Oak Hole Blind . . .

And so it goes.

Finally, we drift off to our rooms, spartan compared to the dining room and living quarters, lit by a single candle or maybe a kerosene lamp with extra wick in the bureau drawer. The pan of wash water will have skim ice on it the next morning. Under a featherbed, we fight for territorial rights with the 90-pound Lab crowding our feet and doze off quickly to the tune of the wind on the eaves.

Morning comes early. About 4:00 a.m., a knock comes at the door: "Mr. Smith, breakfast in a half hour, and she's makin' weather out, Sir." The knock and the same, muffled greeting is repeated down the hallway to the last bedroom.

We dress quickly and head for the fireplace, now ablaze, to join the rest of the regulars. The air is electric as we talk now not of business, but of the day's shooting to come. Coffee followed by a breakfast of wheatcakes, eggs and home-cured sausage with buttermilk biscuits is quickly put away, with the extra going to the big, hard-working black and yellow dogs that seem to have adopted the spots to the immediate right of their masters.

Then, we all clamber into the "mud room" where the forearms and barrels on the Parkers are clicked into place. By mutual agreement, maybe even unspoken, the members all shoot doubles. The fairly new repeating shotguns—pumps and autoloaders—are not accepted here. Maybe someone is using one of the little 12-gauges, but most of us have chosen our 10s—maybe even an 8-gauge. Pockets are stuffed with shells, and we head out the door for the boats and the blinds. No need to worry about putting out decoys—Eustus set out the blocks in the last failing light of Friday night. They will be picked up Sunday evening and not set out again until the following weekend, unless a member takes a shooting vacation of a week or 10 days at the club.

There are no young men here, not even any member's children present. The club is exclusive. A member can will his place in the club to an heir, but so far the members' numbers have been undiminished by death. The club is as it was when it was founded, thank God.

Poling the boat to the blind in the starlight, we hear the quacking of ducks on the water. Puddlers. The blind we are heading for is on the open bay, and canvasbacks are the ducks we're hoping for. Pushing the boat into the blind, we take up watch, you to the left and I to the right.

About the time you can count the eyelets in your boots, the first flight of cans sweeps low over the water, rises to get a look at the blocks, makes one more pass, and then bores in.

We rise. My 10-gauge passes the lead duck and I slap the front trigger. The third duck in the line pinwheels into the water, so hard he skips like a flat stone on a pond. Pulling still farther ahead, I trigger the left barrel. The copper-plated 4s take the bird in full flight, and he joins his flockmate on the water. Your two shots have pulled a pair from the rear of the flock, your appointed area because the birds entered from the left—your side.

The dogs are sent out, and they locate the ducks bobbing lifelessly among the Mason decoys. Two trips for each dog and the birds are tucked away inside the blind. Like us, our dogs work as a well-oiled team.

Hunkered down in the blind, we wait for the next flight. All thoughts of business and civilization are gone now. Our world is a small pole blind and a spread of decoys.

The ducks come screaming in from my side. We can tell they aren't going to stop—they are just strafing the blocks. "Now," you hiss. I stand and swing as fast as I can, but both rounds splash the water behind the tailender. I couldn't quite catch up. Your left barrel took the final, departing duck, and we chuckle at the speed of downwind cans. No matter; there will be more targets soon.

And so it goes. More than 50 times this day, we will squint

down the swamped ribs of our Parkers. By the time Eustus poles up, we have as much shooting as we want. The spanking east wind has carried a hint of snow all day, and now it comes. Men, dogs, decoys and dead canvasbacks are covered in a silent pall of white.

Into the boat now, we pole back to the lodge. The other members are already there, and the good talk commences again. Shots made and missed are relived as the peach brandy loosens inhibitions and tongues.

The call to dinner, a nightcap with a good cigar and then off to bed for the rest we'll need for the Sunday shooting.

That's how I see myself—and you.

Today, you and I worry about droughts on the Canadian prairies, about pesticide accumulations, about farming practices that drain potholes, about what the U.S. Army Corps of Engineers has up its sleeve.

We attend Ducks Unlimited dinners and buy prints. We buy coffee mugs with duck heads on them, and we dream the old dreams. But the old days—there and then—are gone.

Today, you and I are more likely to be fighting a crowd around the game division outpost that holds sway over the public marsh. Our license numbers are recorded, we enter a blind-draw lottery, our guns are checked for plugs, our shells tested with a magnet to make sure that they hold only steel, and our olive-drab canoe is checked for the state registration sticker.

If we get chosen, we set out our own spread of decoys—a dozen or two—and wait for a few mallards or pintails to drift by. We start by the watch and end by it because we have to be out of the area in time to give those who have drawn our blind for the afternoon hunt a chance to set up. All very official, all very friendly, all very much like a herd of cattle shipped from point A to point B.

All very dreary. Except for one thing: When you and I rise to shoot, we may not be looking down between the tubes of a Parker, and the ducks we swing on aren't canvasbacks, but the feeling is there—the surge as you hiss, "Now!"

Sure, we may be sighting along the rib of a production-grade 12-gauge pump, and the shells may hold steel shot, and the ducks may be some unwary greenheads fresh from the North, but the retrieve is just as proud, the burned powder smells the same, and the wind and sleet that sting our faces feel the same to us here and now as they did there and then.

And in the end, isn't that reason enough for us to be here—now?

The passing of these old days is not without some semblance of guilt for the sportsmen of that era. Although I use the term "sportsmen" a bit loosely, these men, many of them converted—reformed—market gunners, were among the first to see the awful impact that unlimited fall and spring shooting had on the hordes of waterfowl.

Yet, they themselves would surely be regarded as game hogs if they tried to pull off some of those old game bags today. They would probably be visited only on alternate Tuesdays by a close relative, too.

The market-gunning period, especially for waterfowl, was a period of plenty for an emerging nation. Some have wondered about the mentality of those who operated punt guns, shot at night, or snared and trapped birds and animals for the market. The answer is obvious—and easy: money. A partial price listing of poultry and wildfowl sold on the market 100 years ago from an outlet in Baltimore shows that geese went for $2 a pair in those days.

If you think about it, $2 100 years ago may have represented one week's pay for a laborer working all day. One shot at a flock of geese could make a man comfortable, for a time, by those standards. The canvasback—at $5 to $7 a brace—could make a man rich.

Some of the early gunners, plying their craft on the Chesapeake or Hudson, or the Great Lakes, had flotillas of boats, decoy pick-up men, and may have looked down between the barrels of a double 500 times a day or more. A good fall or spring shooting season made the market hunter an economic force to be reckoned with in his community.

The Susquehanna River, and particularly the Susquehanna Flats, was an area that provided a living for quite a few gunners. They came for the "sport," as they saw it, but they came primarily for the cash. As late as the 1890s, newspapers sent reporters to the Flats to cover the opening week's gunning. Amazing.

An examination of the hunting regulations in effect in the United States in the late 1920s shows that this country was a nation of waterfowlers. While some of the great grouse and woodcock states such as Michigan, Wisconsin and Minnesota had yet to open a legal season on grouse, and had only a five-day season for woodcock and "imported pheasant," most states held waterfowl shooting from mid-September until mid-December.

Little wonder, then, that ducks and geese took the brunt of the shooting by the early sportsmen. Many of these men organized and became the early advocates of seasons and bag limits. They recognized that the market shooting of the past was just that—in the past. They lobbied for imposition of season lengths and bag limits, and eventually they were the ones who pressed for an end to the use of live decoys and a beginning of waterfowl management via duck stamp monies.

Still, their bags were impressive. Shooters of the Great Lakes areas and points east used to rent train cars and once a year make a foray to the western prairies for some of the Central Flyway shooting in the open spaces. These trips, many of them for two months at a time, featured paid cooks, helpers, duck-pluckers and probably valets who made sure the shooter looked right before he headed out in the morning.

Every major city near a body of water that held waterfowl sported its own ducking club, like that described earlier, and the shooters were often as social and politically-conscious as they were aware of how far ahead to hold on a downwind redhead. Detroit, for example, with the St. Clair River nearby, was a hotbed of shooting in the 20s.

But with the Dustbowl days of the 30s came a new consciousness born of lean years. Those days robbed the prairies of their duck-giving waterholes, and it was clear that the glory years had gone by. It was time for the legislation that would pass all of the old days into the mists of time.

Bag limits became set more tightly: the season lengths became shorter and started to vary from year to year. Federal laws took precedence over what a state wanted to do. A resource that moves across state lines quacking or honking was better regulated by the feds.

At the same time, the upland hunting picture was changing.

Pheasants, successfully introduced in the late 1800s, drew followers who figured that a pretty and good-tasting bird *had* to be worth some time. Grouse and woodcock became more common as the market-hunting laws and land use made their populations burgeon. Season lengths stretched out in the uplands at the time when those on waterfowl were shortening. Many waterfowlers simply moved inland, away from the waters, and started hunting upland birds. The interest in wetland hunting slowed.

The coming of the Federal Refuge system, financed in great part by duck stamp monies, was an attempt to combat, in this country, the duck and goose's worst enemy—loss of habitat. Still, unlike many species of game, ducks and geese are especially prone to hunting as a predatory factor. There are now disturbing reports that there are far fewer ducks returning north to nest each year than there should be. The habitat for nesting, in many cases, could support many more birds than are using it, and biologists are starting to wonder out loud if shooting isn't hurting the populations more than they had reckoned. Time will tell.

The decline in numbers of waterfowlers is also something that alarms those who make their salaries by duck-stamp money. Too little reward for too much equipment and time may be the reason for this situation. What with the cost of clothing, boats, motors, decoys, a Lab or two, calls and steel shot, a pair of mallards on a good day isn't enough to make some people plunk down their cash on a stamp and try their luck.

This circle becomes a cycle: fewer hunters, less money, fewer ducks, fewer hunters . . . Damn.

But, there is some good news. The advent of steel shot laws, a general feeling of environmental awareness, tougher pollution laws and the system of refuges are going to combine to bring back waterfowl. Organizations such as Ducks Unlimited and the growth of state waterfowl organizations are going to help the birds they already have. The name of the game is money—the more the better for waterfowl. Managing for ducks is expensive. Areas have to be diked and flooded, water levels controlled, the birds have to be protected during the molt when they can't fly, wardens have to be paid, as do the biologists, and fields have to be sharecropped with feed for the birds in mind. It makes grouse and quail management look like a picnic by comparison.

Another piece of good news is the goose population on this continent. This topic will be explored a little more fully in Chapter 4, which deals with these majestic birds, but suffice it to say that these creatures have probably never been healthier as species than right now. Nesting far enough north so that the bulldozers haven't turned their grounds into shopping centers yet, they use the refuges to their advantage and, indeed, there may be as many geese now as there was before white men started popping caps at them.

A final piece of good news concerns the mettle of the men who gun the flocks. As time goes along, the sportsmanship of the camouflaged clan seems to be getting better with each season. There are fewer skyshooters, fewer illegal "hunters," fewer incidences of having to be the first on the water or the first away from the launch site. The companionships that can form in a refuge parking lot are the kind made of something good, and solid, and right—a belief in the sporting ethic and a fondness for the birds we hunt.

This may be the best news of all.

2

The Divers

If I could give a color to diver-duck shooting, and I can because I'm writing this book, I'd color it blue.

Blue is the color of the bill of the most popular diver ducks since the canvasback and redhead started to go the route of the bison, the whooping crane and 32 cents a gallon gas. I'm talking about bluebills (lesser scaup) and broadbills (greater scaup). These two species are the mainstay of diver shooters today, and probably for years to come. Nesting farther north and west than either cans or redheads, they are less likely to be disturbed by some guy with the IQ of a fence rail and the keys to a bulldozer.

Besides heavy overshooting for the market, the canvasback and redhead became victims of several forces that conspired to

9

put them down for the count. First, they taste almost too good. Secondly, they were almost too trusting. A good stool of blocks and a few toots on your call to get their attention, and you were in business. Thirdly, they are a wingshooter's ultimate test. Trying to hit a downwind can is extremely challenging and difficult; doing so is a noteworthy feat.

Unfortunately, nesting grounds too close to the population centers of the United States was the ultimate enemy of the canvasback and redhead. The scaups don't have that problem—at least they won't until some infidel in a business suit decides that a K-mart can be built on top of permafrost.

Blue is also the color that we associate with the fingers of your typical diver hunter on your typical diver hunting day. The best days to hunt these birds is when the weather conditions place the human participants very near to death. You can literally die of exposure in a deep-water bluebill blind. If you tip over out there, make sure you've named your executor.

Divers are tough, too. Up where they live, snow and ice are facts of life practically all year long, so they really won't move down until freeze-up comes and the food supply turns white. Because of this, many states have extended seasons to let shooters get in on the late-migrating scaup. These bonus birds are often liberally limited in the game laws, too. While the mallard hunter often enjoys his shooting on naive, young birds in sometimes bluebird weather, the diver hunter has his inning when his fingers turn to stovewood, his nose is but a memory, and his toes are a cruel joke.

The Midwest, especially the Great Lakes, gets its share of diver shooting, but the coasts, especially the East, are the strongholds of the diving-duck clan: bluebills, broadbills, scoters, goldeneyes (whistlers), ringnecks (ringbills), buffleheads (butterballs), ruddy ducks and the mergansers ("fish ducks").

To put it bluntly, in my opinion the divers are not what you could call "overly-intellectually gifted." Compared to some gun-educated mallards or those wary spooks, black ducks, most of the divers, even in heavily-gunned areas, are a shade or two above a box of rocks in the smarts department. Still, you have to know what you're doing to take limits of these birds and stay alive in the process.

Divers are also the birds of lore and legend. In his mind's

eye, the hunter of today sees himself braving the elements, squinting into the distance to catch that first flash of underbelly as the birds streak out of the leaden, snow-spitting sky and make their first sonic blast over his blocks. He stands, thumbs the safety off his vintage double, and pulls a pair of drakes from the front of the knot and grins grimly as his Lab or Chessie hits the surf. His steel-gray eyes flicker toward the horizon as he notes wind speed and direction, and plans his next pair.

Nowhere does he imagine lugging three metric tons of decoys into a leaky boat with a motor that hasn't run properly since the Truman Administration. In his imagination, the cold is there, but it isn't "real." His dog gets every bird and never shakes inside the blind. You and I know what things are really like, but we aren't talking. There still might be someone out there willing to go with us if we keep our mouths shut.

Depending upon the game laws, layout shooting is one of the most exciting sports this side of the town where the bulls chase the Spanish kids through the streets. Layout shooting is aptly named for several reasons, the first of which is the fact that the participants in this little drama could just as easily be "laid out" in a casket in a funeral parlor.

The second is the fact that it is really named for the position the shooter takes in the boat, which is a low, sneakbox type of

Two men share a layout boat. Hunting divers in this manner requires a second craft to act as a tender. Photo by Steven Griffin.

craft. He literally lies down in the thing, and, except for this cover is "naked before his enemies." A "tender" boat to carry decoys, pick up the birds, and haul what's left of the shooter back to shore rounds out the equipment. Because you need a tender, this is a two-man activity, but only one of the crazies shoots at a time.

Because of the duck's habits, layout shooting is practiced on big waters: coastal bays, some of the Great Lakes and wide rivers such as the Susquehanna. Diver ducks feed on vegetation about 60 percent of the time, with wild celery being the favored food. They dive deep, using their feet only for propulsion, and even their physical structure is geared for this. Where the dabbler or puddle duck has its legs closer to the center of the body, using its middle section as a fulcrum to bend over, the diver's feet are located well back, making walking on land difficult, but making deep dives a thing of ease.

Thus, the best way to hunt divers is by going offshore. Sure, you'll get mixed puddler/diver bags as each invades the other's habitat from time to time, but the layout shooter knows what he's about: late in the year, offshore, cold water, lots of depth, I gotta have my head read.

Shooting from a layout boat is a lot like trying to hit the rabbits at the carnival shooting gallery—while you're riding the ferris wheel. The layout boat is stable but subject to the whims of the tides and the wind.

There you are. You're flat on your back, your shotgun across your chest in a port-arms position. You know there was a time in your life when you had toes, but you're sure they're gone now. The boat rocks side to side and up and down. The decoys are out there somewhere, many dozens of them. It takes so many to get the attention of divers. You can call if you want, but it's the spread of blocks that will do the trick if, indeed, there is a trick to be done. You start thinking about the point spread in the NFL playoff game or just how bad you should jam things into Uncle Sam on your 1040 this year. Then, you hear the sound of air being sucked through primaries. When the sound is that close, the birds are there and in range.

Now you have to decide. Do you wait and hope the birds make another pass? Do you sit and try to locate them based

upon sound alone? You haven't seen any of the bluebills overhead, so they must be out in front of you where the two lines
of decoys converge, leaving that "sweet spot" opening that all
diver hunters like to have within good shotgun range.

You decide to wait. You try to run the data through your
mental computer: speed and declination of the quarry, the boat-
bounce factor, the ribbing your partner will give you if you let
two passes go by without shooting, how far out the birds are
likely to be, and does your left arm still work?

Then you are up, sitting bolt upright in the craft. You see
them, now, at the same time they see you. In the time it takes
you to move inches, they are putting yards of altitude and distance between you. The Model 12 cracks off a round, the wind
steals the sound of the big magnum load. A bird drops. You work
the slide and slap the trigger again. Another bird. A third shot
punches air. You are dimly aware that the chase boat has its
motor started and the dead birds are already the subject of discussion between your partner and his Lab. They pick up the
birds, head over, and the two of you gingerly trade places. You
sit in the tender boat for awhile, talking with him, reliving the
shots in case he missed some minute detail. You tell him how
you had to allow forward and under because the boat was really
rocking. At no time do you mention that you hit two birds at
the opposite end of the flock from where you were pointing. You
light your pipe and make sure all your parts work, then you
motor away to give your partner his privacy—his own private
little piece of frozen heaven.

Layout shooting may be the most exciting form of duck
hunting on the continent, but it's certainly not the most unusual.
One of the odder ways to hunt divers is with—or from—a sinkbox. In this form of shooting, a 55-gallon drum is weighted so
that it will stay on the bottom in a few feet of water, with only
a few inches of freeboard sticking up. The shooter then hops
inside and waits, hunkered low.

The sinkbox is usually located right among the decoys, and
is virtually invisible to any birds coming in unless they come in
right overhead. Even then, they still probably won't know what
you are. A sinkbox is a chilly operation, and sudden squalls can
make your carcass an immediate part of the local aquatic eco-

system, and it takes a tender boat, much like layout shooting, but the rewards can be great.

Layout shooting and sinkbox shooting are not the mainstays of this sport, of course. For divers, the deepwater blind setup is what kills birds. The blind in question is usually the boat itself, with the appropriate amount of netting and reeds to conceal the occupants.

In such a situation, it's a good idea to take as many decoys as you can haul. The best way is to have a separate boat loaded with blocks to tow to the set-up area.

In the matter of decoy material, the heavier the better, within reason. Heavy decoys (cedar, cork) sway in the wind less, roll less, and, in general, look a little more like ducks than do the plastic models.

Patterns for laying out the spread go by a variety of names: the "J," the "Fishhook" and so forth. The main thing to remember is that you want to give the ducks two impressions. First, you have to convince them that there is food down there in the deep. Divers, unlike puddle ducks, have a tendency to knot up more when feeding. This is probably because the food, when present, is in the form of a submerged aquatic weedbed. To effectively work such a bed, the ducks naturally bunch up. They also tend to travel in bigger flocks than puddlers, so the decoys should be bunched.

The second impression you have to give the birds is that there is a safe and inviting place to land when they choose to make a pass. Arranging the blocks in the Fishoook or J pattern leaves an opening that the birds will, hopefully, gravitate to. By placing the shank of the hook downwind with the bend of the hook upwind, you subliminally tell the ducks, "Okay, come in against the wind, as I know you like to. Fly along the shank of the hook until you've reached the area where the bend starts. Once there, you probably won't cross over the end of the shank but will, instead, put out your webbed feet, backpedal and sit down." Or something like that. You may just deviously chuckle, "Hee, hee, hee" and let it go at that. It's up to you.

In deepwater blinds, another set that can work well is to cluster a large number (almost a "google") of decoys around the blind except in the front, where you should leave an opening

Watching the skies in comfort. This permanent, deep-water blind affords luxury not normally found in waterfowling where the main contest might consist of staying alive. Photo by Steven Griffin.

well within shotgun range. The birds will most likely come to that opening. Again, happy divers (those filling their bellies) cluster up, so remember that.

When divers make their first pass at the blocks, it's up to you what to do. Some groups bust straight in and sit down. Others pass once or twice before coming in. Some pass once or twice and then buzz away. Others come in low and fast, like fighters on a strafing run, and keep on going with afterburners lit.

I like to have it well set with my partners what we are going to do. I've hunted with fellows who will shoot at anything close, others who insist that all flocks be waited out even if they are in range, in the belief that they will come in with legs spread like a David Maass painting. Some days, no ducks will decoy to any spread, so you have to adjust.

In both diver and dabbler shooting, this is the moment of truth. Never believe the man who says he can tell what the ducks are going to do before they do it. Most days, the ducks don't even know until it happens. Do you wait and hope they come in? Do you take them on the first pass? Do you wait for two passes?

One workable solution is to give the birds the first swing to look you over and make up what passes for their minds. If they haven't decided by the second go-round, take them if they're in range.

Depending on what the birds are doing, you will probably have to alter this arrangement somewhat. If they are decoying well, you can wait them out; a lot of that depends upon the weather. If they are in the mood for buzzing some fine day, you may be reduced to pass shooting them as they go from point A to point B and you happen to be in the way.

Charlie Lichon, my ducking partner, is great at giving me the business about "We shoulda waited," or "We shoulda taken them" all in the same breath, sometimes. Under pressure, he grins his easy grin and allows as how he doesn't have any better idea than anybody else. If the ducks are in the air, they're thinking it over. If they're gone or on the water, they've made up their minds. If you're looking for wisdom, you'll find it right after "Wisconsin" in the dictionary.

A string of diver decoys starting at a point of land and heading into deeper water. Divers often seem to love to buzz such points, and the strings of blocks influence them toward the blind. Photo by Steven Griffin.

Good watercraft are essential for diver duck shooting. A deep-V boat of at least 16 feet makes me feel pretty safe, although 14 feet is probably fine. A good kicker of at least 5 h.p. gets you out and—more important—gets you back with less time on the water.

This type of waterfowling also demands the right type of clothing. More on that later, but at the very least each person should be equipped with a flotation device. Some of the new vests offer protection without hindering gun fit and mounting. At the least, always wear them when the craft is moving.

Calling in diver hunting is really a matter of getting the attention of the birds. The arrangement and number of decoys is more important. To a great extent this is the opposite of puddle duck hunting, where a good caller can make or break a day. I know diver shooters who regularly wave a hanky or their hand once or twice to get the birds to notice the blocks. Try *that* with black ducks once! I told you divers weren't avian geniuses.

If you're thinking about trying this sport, but are holding back for some reason, let me go over possible reasons for your hesitation. I think part of the problems associated with diver hunting these days revolve around the effort and outlay it takes to hunt them in the "grand manner" of the past.

Lots of decoys, a good, stout boat capable of handling heavy seas, a hunt-toughened dog and the dangers of being a long way from land in terrible weather are probably too much for many average waterfowlers today.

In addition, there is competition from other sports—deer hunting, for one—when the diver shooting gets really good, which is to say late in the season.

Deepwater blinds are tough to construct—naturally they are essentially part of the boat and expensive as well. But when the birds are flying, or when the storms have finally moved them down from the north, there's nothing like it.

The places where you hunt these birds are also quite special. For the serious diver-duck hunter, the Promised Land is Canada. Here, on some of the Prairie lakes, diver hunting is as it once was, and a shooting trip there takes on the proportions of a lifetime hunt.

Goldeneyes, scaup, ringnecks, canvasbacks, buffleheads and

redheads have been known—and are known—there in numbers that can only be imagined in the States. This is primarily because the three major flyways join in Canada. Once into the States, the birds disperse along these migrational corridors.

Three lakes and a marsh come to mind when I think of diver hunting in Canada: Lake Winnepegosis (122 miles long), Lake Winnepeg (260 miles), Lake Manitoba (119 miles) and the Delta Marsh (36,000 acres). These are big areas, with huge populations of divers.

Here, they say, flocks are measured in the time it takes them to pass overhead, and the limits are more liberal than stateside gunners are used to.

Naturally, the stubblefield hunting for puddlers, especially mallards that fatten on spilled wheat, normally takes the attention of out-of-country gunners, but the diver shooting can be phenomenal. Alberta, Manitoba and Saskatchewan all offer waterfowl shooting of the first water, but the chance to shoot divers as they once were hunted is the lure that calls many southern gunners north to the big country. Remember, most divers decoy less readily early in the season. After things cool off a bit, they are more likely to stool. If you wait for this time, though, you could potentially be too late for the great waves of birds because cold snaps and fronts will have shuttled them south. It's a chance you take with any out-of-state hunting, but even if you miss the main hordes, there are usually plenty of birds around right up until freeze-up.

3

The Dabblers

If the bluebill is the mainstay of diver shooting, then the throne of most popular dabbling duck goes to the mallard. Nothing will stir the imagination of a waterfowler more than the sight of a flock of greenheads dropping into the decoys right after shooting time starts. No duck is more widespread nor more recognizable than the mallard, either. School kids who wouldn't know a swan from a Swahili can tell you that the ducks they feed in the park on Sunday are mallards.

The mallard and its first cousin, the black, are the birds that stir the soul. They are good eating, and they are wary—true prizes when taken fairly. There is also a rather large assortment of ways to bring them, as the game department lads say, "to possession."

The story of the mallard in the United States is the story of the federal- and state-managed public hunting areas, at least to a great extent.

Not long ago, I was returning from a trip to Texas to my native Michigan. Coming from Detroit to Saginaw in the darkness, the airplane was about half full of equally exhausted business travelers. The drone of the jet engines further added to the hypnosis of the moment. The lights of one city blended into those of the next. The sensation hit me that always hits me when I'm on airplanes, that someone created a perfect living and working model of the earth and placed it outside the window just for my amusement.

South of Saginaw, and as the plane started its descent, I saw a huge black glob—a void. That void was, I knew, the Shiawassee Flats National and State Wildlife Refuge, the home of thousands of ducks and geese and several hundred species of assorted furry creatures and dickey-birds. I had flown over the place in daylight on the way to Texas and had noticed the winding rivers, the oxbows where the watercourses cut new paths, the flooded cropfields, and the dead and dying forests, the water levels spelling their doom.

But in the dark, I imagined I was a goose flying down from the subarctic nesting grounds, navigating by the stars. I imagined I was a mallard, coming back from an afternoon feeding binge in a neighboring field. That great glob of darkness that was the Flats was home, a haven. There, civilization was a bad memory. City stacks and concrete ribbons didn't intrude, and I was safe, genetically remembering the earth as it once was.

Below, and in season, the hunters could come with their 12-gauge shotguns, but here I had an even chance. There were places—the refuge sections—where they could not get to me. Even the hunters' guns were limited in number, restricted to certain areas, limited to a box of shells, and those shells had to hold steel shot. How good it was, I thought, to be duck or goose and see that chasm before me.

The managed areas are, more than likely, the hunting of the

future. Supported in large part with hunters' money, they are planned with waterfowl in mind. Hunting is strictly controlled, and the sporting experience is what matters. Those with dogs are given preferential treatment in some cases, and hunters are not jammed together.

The areas, typically, feature a variety of habitats. Flooded crops where the birds can feed, flooded woods for resting, river habitats in some cases, shorelines in others, and usually miles of cattails studded with potholes. The refuge area is well managed and well patrolled, as it should be.

Getting an area to hunt usually means drawing a blind or an area where you can fashion one if no permanent structure exists. This is done by a lottery system whereby the guilty all queue up in the predawn hours, take a number and then choose an area to hunt based upon what's left when their number comes up. Two to four people per blind is the norm, and you take a number for your party. The draw is usually held a couple of hours before shooting time, which gives you plenty of time to get to your car, drive to a launch site, get lost in the dark and finally get set up.

Most places offer morning and afternoon hunts so twice as many people can take part. In the afternoon, it's the same deal—figuratively, you pays your money and you draws your cards.

The folks who run these places are good about telling everyone before the draw what the field and water conditions are like, whether there are "new birds" (migrants fresh from the north), what fields and blinds have been producing, the rules and regulations, and anything else they can do to help you have a good time.

For their part, the hunters are pretty good about checking in with the kill data so that accurate records can be kept. They are also trying to be well-mannered about the whole thing. Outside of the odd dogfight in the parking lot, the draw is usually uneventful. Normally, I'm so far toward the last drawn that one time the blind they gave me was in Nepal. If you get a high pick and guess right about where the birds are working, you can have a dandy time.

Picking an area to hunt is usually chancy and depends on what fields have been producing—like which field produced yesterday. It's a good idea to have a first, second, and third choice,

A happy waterfowler with a drake mallard, the most popular and abundant of the puddle ducks. Calls and decoy arrangements for mallards will lure virtually all of the dabbler species. Photo by Steven Griffin.

because some other sharpie will slicker you if he gets drawn first. But even if you don't get a choice area, you still could do well because conditions and pressure can send the birds almost anywhere in the legal hunting area—or keep them inside the refuge.

A few tricks can make things a little easier, however. When the migration is on and fresh ducks are coming in, especially if there is a spanking north wind to push them, locating on the northern edge of the managed area is a good bet. The birds, down from the north, see the area, spot your blocks and pitch in, tired but happy. With luck, they'll leave some of their number behind.

Ducks will feed heavily prior to a big front. As the season progresses and the food supply dwindles at the same time that the ducks are trying to store up winter fat, hunting cropfields with remnants of feed still available can produce.

During really lousy weather, the birds will often make for the refuge area itself. Several times I've had good shoots by using a huge number of oversized decoys right on the edge of the refuge—as close as legally possible. Ducks coming in overhead knew that they were close to safety, saw my blocks, figured those lads down there had things sorted out, geographically, and dropped in. God, it was ugly.

At other times, especially early in the season, flooded timber is a good bet. Ducks use this as a combination feeding/loafing area, especially during the "lull."

The "lull" is the time of the season when the shooting slackens. The managed areas are also topflight nesting areas, and many birds rear their young right there—native birds. As the season progresses, those natives that aren't shot become damn well educated. At this time, and before the migration brings in fresh birds, the shooting can get a little slim. At such times, blinds that no one has used, especially near flooded timber, can produce.

The word inevitably gets around as to which blinds and fields are producing birds. Because of heavy pressure on these spots, especially on weekends, your best bet is on weekdays. Strangely enough, really good duck hunting weather (which means it's lousy anything-else weather) on the weekend produces few hunters.

The success rate at these managed areas speaks well of the places as hunting havens. The numbers of ducks shot per hunter hour are far and away above what the average hunter can expect if he goes the find-your-own-place-to-hunt route. Too, the private lands surrounding such areas are like gold, and the shooting rights are usually leased up tight with agreements forged in blood. This is especially true if the managed area holds geese as well as ducks.

For the most part, puddle ducks are the dominant species, with some divers as an aside. Shooters hunting these areas can plan for both, but you're wiser if you set up for mallards, blacks, pintails or one of the other dabbler species.

Before getting into blinds, decoy rigs, boats and the other minutiae, let's take a look at the shooting opportunities that most of us have right under our bills for puddle ducks—maybe without realizing it.

Anywhere ducks migrate, there will be water available. Sometimes that water is small and hidden, sometimes it's an ocean coastline. But if you're hunting dabblers, prospecting can also pay big bonuses (bonusi?).

After the shooting starts, many birds start to look for safe havens to feed, cavort, make lewd remarks to the females and generally carry on. Such places can be unseen potholes, rivers, streams or stock ponds. Locating places where the birds are congregating, especially native birds, is a fascinating late-summer activity; sort of pre-season scouting.

Years ago, a pal and I had good luck gunning three farm ponds that all held ducks. In those days, we were terrible shots as opposed to today when we are merely lousy. Consequently, we smartened up more birds than we took home, but that was okay. Hope springs eternal and all like that. We would start our day sequestered in the cattails of Pond A, waiting for shooting time. When the appointed minute came, we would leap up. About 40 or 50 ducks, mostly mallards, would leap up, too, and we'd blaze away, Partner and I. Well, that was our ducking for the day, usually, until we discovered that the ducks were going over one section line to another, similar pond, Pond B. This pond had an embankment that two lithe and supple lads could use for cover as we Indianed our way up to the water's edge. Again, *surprise*.

We discovered Pond C quickly because we had, by now, deduced that the ducks were merely making a circuit from pond to pond. We did the same.

How well I remember one day in late October when Partner and I took in a crony for *The Plan*. This was conceived to be the ultimate. Using two sets of decoys, Partner and Crony were to take up positions on Ponds B and C, respectively, with the blocks out. I was to be at Pond A awaiting the sun. When I jumped and shot, the reasoning went, the birds would fly to B where Partner would ambush them as they decoyed. Crony was to bushwhack them when they hightailed it from B to C. With luck, Crony's shooting would send them back to A.

All went as planned. I could hear the others shooting after I'd had my usual fortune of missing everything that got off the water. Later, when we reconvened, we found that The Plan had worked, we had all seen ducks, we'd all had shots, and we didn't have one duck. Too bad.

Even though the moral of this little story may be a trifle obscure, I learned from it. Ducks show up in some unlikely places, but there's normally a reason why they are there, and some method in it, after a fashion.

One of the best aids for scouting likely potholes is a set of topographical maps. These are available from the U. S. Geologic Survey in Washington, D. C., and they come in quadrangles for most of the country. There are two sizes, but get the 7½-minute size. These are more detailed, showing small lakes or ponds that may be off the beaten track.

I grouse hunt quite a bit. Once, while using the maps to locate grouse coverts, I noted a small lake that was unnamed on my map. My setter and I hiked over toward it. We knew we were close when we saw some dead, still-standing trees. We soon jumped, and I shot, a nice brace of teal. The pond was actually the backwaters of a beaver pond that had probably existed, off and on, for decades. By the way, I went back the following spring and caught some brook trout, too.

These maps have a lot of detail to them—enough to warrant the expense of buying them. One of their interesting features is that they show intermittent streams. These are usually water courses that are functioning only when the water is high, like when there is spring runoff. But the intriguing thing is that many times these intermittent streams, shown as broken lines on the topo map, have pools of water in low areas where the flowage collected and did not run off. These small pools, if they are large enough for a duck to swim around in the middle where he feels safe from shorebound predators, are often worth checking out.

The beautiful thing about such prospecting is that it requires nothing more than the proper licenses and stamps, a gun and a good pair of boots. If your dog will stay at heel until needed to retrieve, take him along too. If he won't, teach him.

Jump shooting can also take the form of simply getting away from a shore blind for a while and tramping about. Now "tramping about" in cattails while wearing a pair of chest waders may seem a little masochistic, but it sure gets the blood moving.

Once, my aforementioned pal Charlie and I were having little luck at a river blind set in a sea of cattails. Charlie decides to take a hike. Pretty soon, I hear him shoot. He shoots again. When he had fired on three separate occasions, I hiked back too. He was jump shooting mallards in tiny potholes in the openings in the cattails and having a ball doing it. I helped him.

Another time Charlie, Dave Oeming and I were in the middle of a big blow with no ducks moving. To keep his call from freezing up, Dave took a few tentative toots. A duck answered back. It sounded like a Suzy, so Dave took his yellow Lab back for a look, thinking it to be a cripple. Charlie and I watched as the duck swam out of the flooded corn, toward the blocks, and flushed—the only duck we saw all day.

When setting out your decoys, remember that flooded areas often hold small openings in the vegetation which are natural places to set a block or two. Such isolated decoys make it look, from the air, that here, below, is a very contented flock of waterfowl spread about the open water (your main body of decoys) and the reeds (the single decoys) calmly feeding and why don't we just drop in for dinner?

In fact, when setting out dabbler decoys, remember that these ducks are more likely to be spread out than divers would be. Dabblers bunch together when they are frightened or extremely wary. From the air, spread out dabbler decoys give the impression of safety and comfort.

I like to use an opening—not a J rig as I would for divers—but an opening between loose groups of decoys. The intention is for the birds to come right at you in your blind and set down in the opening. To make this happen, you have to have the wind at your back, if you can. If you can't, then have the wind at your side so that birds passing into the wind will offer you crossing shots. This is the second most deadly shot on a duck, the first being straight on where you get an excellent chance to put shot into the head and neck.

Many hunters use a few goose decoys as confidence builders. There's something about a few Canadas away from the main body of decoys that tends to bring ducks in a little more readily. The big birds are very wary, and their presence probably indicates that all is well down there.

Place your goose decoys, with some feeding and at least one with head erect, out from the blind about 40 to 45 yards. Not only is this where they would be found if they were to be cohabiting with ducks, it's also an excellent way to gauge the range of incoming birds; when they come in over the geese, they're in range.

I like to use as many decoys as I can lug—or get someone else to lug—to the marsh. The plastic models are good enough for puddlers, because you seldom have to put up with the wind and tide currents so prevalent in offshore gunning. If you are flaring birds, try tying heavy monofilament line onto your anchors instead of the usual black braided stuff or the thicker twine, especially if the water is abnormally clear.

Make sure that the paint on the decoys is at least in keeping with the species you expect to be shooting, and mix in a few pintail blocks, with their lighter colors, to help draw attention to your spread. Make sure that the lines on the blocks are the right length; too short and they'll pull loose, too long and you'll have a tangled mess with decoys bobbing unnaturally with each wavelet.

While on the subject of decoying, let me add that calling is at least as important as the blocks, or that the two should operate in concert. Where the call may attract the attention of divers to the decoys, the dabblers can be enticed in with the right combinations of highballs, chuckles and comebacks. A good man with a call is hard to find.

Calling dabbling ducks, for many hunters, is usually a matter of too much and at the wrong time. I'm a real believer in the fact that the primary use of a call should be to attract attention to the decoy spread. After that, the thing should be put away. It does, of course, take a good hand with a call to get dabblers to even look.

Calling has always been an inexact science. I don't think I'd classify it as an art as some do, simply because in order for it to work, you've got to be able to understand a little about waterfowl mentality. Specifically, you've got to be able to understand when calling will and will not work.

Essentially, there are ducks that are looking to set down, and those who couldn't care less. Rather than screeching away at those who are not interested in you, keep silent. Perhaps those ducks will be amenable to calling at another time—or even another place. The flock that is high and going fast is usually a waste of breath. So, too, is the flock that numbers greater than the decoys you have out. Trying to call 50 mallards into a spread of a dozen blocks is usually a waste of time, unless the weather is really terrible.

Likewise, any high single is normally a bird you're best off letting alone. He usually knows where he's going and what he's going there for. Let him be.

The low single and small flocks—again, those traveling low— are prime calling targets. Use a highball to attract their attention, a feeding chuckle when they're close and a comeback if they seem to lose interest. Two men can sound like a flock if they know which end of the call makes the noise. One highballing and one chuckling can do the trick on birds that may be decoy-shy.

Trying to reach out-of-earshot birds often throws off both the cadence and the pitch of your calling. It's similar to trying to sing "Ave Maria" at the top of your lungs; it just doesn't get the job done.

But, once birds are headed your way and you see the first tentative setting of the wings, put away the call. They've seen

the blocks and are headed in. The insistence that some hunters
have for calling right until the birds hit the water will frequently
flare birds that otherwise would have set down. Real ducks won't
call that much after they've sensed that the newcomers have
them spotted, so you shouldn't either.

Not long ago, I was in a blind on a publicly-owned marsh.
The fellows in the blind next to me insisted on trying to call
ducks that were specks over the treetops several miles off. About
all they did was make a lot of commotion, and they didn't convince even one bird to come over for a look-see. Instead, they
just made a lot of motion trying to "throw" the sound as far as
they could.

The wind will play with your calling as well. Birds ap-
proaching from upwind (wind at their rear) have to be hailed
with a little more gusto than those coming the other way. Depending upon whether the wind is carrying the sound to them
or away from them, you will have to adjust—just like real birds
will. Also, if birds are fighting the wind to come in your direction,
you can give the highball and feeding chuckle sooner than you
would if they've got a tailwind. With a good, stiff wind carrying
my calling to them, I break into the chuckle while the ducks are
still 200 to 300 yards off. To them, it sounds pretty loud.

After some experimenting, you'll find that some calls are
specialists. Some brands work the best for hailing, others are in
their prime when giving the feeding chuckle. It's a bother to
switch calls, which is why the two-man calling technique works
best. Each specializes in what he does best with the call that
does it best.

Blind shooting for dabbling ducks can take place from a
canoe, a sneak boat, a deepwater blind or a permanent land blind.
Even a prairie pit blind that a goose hunter would use may be
just what will take the birds at times. But there are a few basics
in the construction of a good blind.

First, concealment. The vegetation that surrounds the blind
should be of the materials native to that area and of the same
age as the surrounding vegetation. Using brown cattails while
gunning early fall teal is a dead giveaway, pardon the expression.
Likewise, cornstalks amongst the reeds will pretty well label you
a beginner.

The blind should allow for freedom of movement to swing and shoot without limiting you to a small "window" field of fire. This is why two men and a dog can share a blind better than three men. If three hunt together, one should get out and stand concealed if at all possible. In shallow water, I'll sit outside a crowded blind on a folding chair.

The blind should allow for a place for the dog to stand and mark falls while staying dry and out of harm's way—and out of the way, period. Some prefer to build a regular platform for the dog. Others, like my pal, Charlie, place boards on the bottom of the canoe for better footing for the dog and to keep her above the inevitable inch or two of water that collects with all the sloshing in and out of the water by hunter and beast.

One of the toughest lessons to learn about duck hunting is blind placement. The best blind in the world with the world's best decoys and a champion caller inside will rarely tempt birds to come where they don't want to go. On any given day, ducks are likely to have chosen a flight pattern, and it's necesary to observe that pattern when choosing the location for your blind. It's a little simplistic to put it in these terms, but I'm going to anyway: Hunt where the ducks are.

Here's an example. When I was a college lad, my pal, John Stevens, and I did a lot of duck shooting when we should have been attending classes. But, we found the relatively uncrowded conditions of a Tuesday morning at the marsh preferable to Western Civilization 101 or whatever it was we were skipping.

We had a good, camouflaged canoe, a nice spread of blocks, John was an able caller and a good shot, and I knew how to carry stuff to the water and back to the car at the end of the day. We were also young and mobile, and it was our mobility that got us birds. We would be on the water before dawn, as is the way of wildfowlers, but we would sit in the canoe, decoys still in the bag, guns still cased. As the sun rose, we'd watch for the movements of flights of ducks trading across the sky.

Once we'd established what we considered was a flight pattern for that day, we'd scurry over to a likely-looking spot and set up. If there were no birds trading, we'd usually set up where they had been moving in the past and hope. Or, we'd bag it and go pheasant hunting. Such is youth.

As I got older, I got lazier, and this pattern slowly ebbed away. But I've gone back to it in recent years, especially if I'm hunting new territory where I can move about. Obviously, if I'm hunting a managed area where I have to choose a spot and stay there, this form of strategy is out. Makes you about as popular with neighboring hunters as a hole in the boat.

Points of land jutting into water are almost always good places to spot a blind. On windy days, when birds are looking for shelter, at least one side of the peninsula will have a lee shore. On bluebird days (when you probably should be home pulling up the tomato plants), ducks will often buzz these points at relatively low altitudes. The point could also indicate a bay nearby, a cove that the birds use for resting during the mid-part of the day. Always check out points.

In cropfields that have been flooded, hunting from a blind can be a tough arrangement. Most attempts at concealment make the concealees stand out like bleeding digits, especially in flooded corn. The best bet is to set decoys out in open water near the corn and then just try your best to stay low in the boat or canoe. Birds passing overhead, if in range, should probably be tried for because they'll have spotted you and will likely flare. If you have poor cover, it's best to take a chance at the birds as soon as they are in range and forget the classic, backpedaling landing into the blocks; it's not likely to happen.

One of the most productive methods of hunting puddle ducks once the guns start barking is to float for them. On rivers near large bodies of water that the birds use, there are often pretty sizable populations of feeding, congregating and resting ducks. As in finding potholes, topo maps are great helps.

Using the maps, locate a river that drains a swamp or flows into a larger body of water, such as a lake or large pond. The streams which drain swamps are great prospects because they are usually slow moving and have the necessary vegetative food supplies to keep ducks interested.

The equipment is fairly minimal: a canoe, a shotgun, some camo clothing, a retriever (there should *always* be a retriever) and a dozen decoys, maybe less, tucked away in a bag. This is a two-man operation, so you'll have to hunt up a partner.

Dropping the canoe in upstream from one car (with the other car positioned at the takeout point downstream), you start your

Floating for ducks takes a minimum of gear—a couple of men, a dog, and a good watercraft are about all that are needed. Photo by Joe Workosky.

float downstream. Each bend in the river is likely to hold ducks because here the water is shallow and slow on one side, and deeper and faster on the other. And here, a little river geology will help.

Where the river bends, the current will cut into the opposite bank, making that part of the river, called the cutbank, deep with a steeper side and faster water. The ducks are not likely to be loafing in that type of water because it takes too much effort for them to stay there against the current. The food is not there, either, because the current doesn't give vegetation a chance to get a foothold.

In dry years when water levels are low, however, the cutbank side of the current may be where the ducks are because that's the only water available. The cutbank side also freezes last late in the season, so that may be the only water available to the birds come late November.

The other side of the bend, where the slow water is, goes

by the name of slipslope. It is here that the water is shallow and submergent and emergent aquatic plants can find root—and that spells food. In a normal year, early in the season, the birds are most likely to be in the slipslope side of the river as you round the bend.

"Rounding the bend" presents a critical decision on the hunters' part: If there are ducks present, what will they do and what should *you* do in reaction to them?

If you stay to the inside of the river (the side that will become the slipslope side at the next bend), you'll come in on the birds before they realize that you're there. Some cattails or other cover attached to your canoe will get you closer before the birds realize that something is, indeed, rotten in Denmark.

If the birds flush at marginal range, it's best to let them go without shooting. These ducks may just go down the river and set up shop again at the next bend. Also, your shots may alarm other ducks you haven't seen downriver. Naturally, if you get within good range, take your shots—that's what you came for. But if the birds are not in good range, let them go: they will likely be downriver a few hundred yards.

One partner controls the canoe from the stern, the other does the shooting from the bow. Two men shooting can prove dangerous as hell, and at the very least makes the guy in the front a little nervous. It's best to simply take turns using whatever criteria you want: switching after each shot, each duck taken or after every half-hour or something. Whatever you decide, agree before you start; otherwise, you can get some bad feelings generated if one guy gets all the shooting, especially if he rubs it in.

Some rivers also have backwaters to them. Ducks will sit in these waters, and they can often be heard splashing and quacking to each other as you float by. As a river cuts its way through the countryside, it will often loop back on itself as it twists and turns. Eventually, the loops will connect and the river will straighten out over the decades and centuries, leaving bends that hold water but aren't part of the main river anywhere. These oxbows are great loafing places for waterfowl.

Wood ducks will often use these areas, which may include flooded timber for feeding, resting and nesting. The woodie, one of America's great waterfowl management success stories, has come back in almost staggering numbers, and wooded rivers are almost sure bets for him anywhere across his range.

In any case, getting out of the canoe and investigating such areas on foot can not only be productive, but it'll also give you a chance to stretch a bit and walk the dog.

If the river or stream you're working has a number of bends in it, you may want to pull in at one and cut across country to the next on foot, jump shooting any birds that may be waiting at the next bend. This works well if you've been floating the same river a lot and the birds have come to associate any floating object with danger.

If you notice ducks trading overhead quite a bit, and you will if there are birds present, you should consider taking out that bag of decoys and setting up for some impromptu blind

A hipper-clad hunter and his Lab out for some jumpshooting. Note the sling on the shotgun makes it easier to carry about when shooting isn't immediately in the offing and frees up hands for carrying other gear. Photo by Joe Workosky.

shooting. Remember to set up the way that is natural for the birds on the river—on the slipslope side in still water. Hide the canoe and sit on the bank. By the time you see the birds and the birds see you, they will probably be in range and there won't be much time to work them with the call, so don't be bashful about calling even if you don't see the birds. I'd stick to the feeding chuckle with an occasional highball in case there are ducks out there you haven't seen yet. Sound carries well in the river corridor, and a good caller can be quite a guy to invite along.

Since hunting is supposed to be recreation, why not make a day of it? Take along a small charcoal grill, coals and a couple of steaks or hamburger patties and do lunch properly. The waterfowler's lunch is often a disaster—one of those brown-paper-sack numbers—and grilling is a nice change of pace from a sandwich you made at 2:00 a.m.

A grill in a good deepwater blind is also a great idea, for that matter. It'll keep you warm, give you something to do if the birds aren't moving, and if you can't brag about what a great shot you are, you can always brag on your cooking. Get the other guy to agree before you feed him, and watch out for the Lab who probably figures those chunks of meat are for him. Labs will normally insist that you share.

Closely related to river hunting is flooded timber shooting. Finding puddle ducks in flooded timber is often a matter of prospecting, especially along rivers, although many publicly owned marshes have stands of flooded woods too. In some southern areas, such as in the famed Stuttgart, Arkansas region, timber shooting is almost a religion.

Here, the call is the key. The birds can be sweet-talked in with a good chuckle after a few highballs. The shooters try like hell to be part of the tree they're leaning against, and the ducks "waffle" their way downward. Most are mallards, with some pintails mixed in. Sloshing the water with your feet creates ripples that flash in the light to the ducks overhead, giving the impression that there's a whole raft of their boys down there filling their bellies on the acorns dropped by the live oaks, a species capable of surviving standing water and producing mast crops.

Timber shooting calls for some fancy gun work. A duck can

cut some fancy figures in the sky once he realizes the jig's up and he's been had. But judging range is easy, and so is judging speed because you have a reference point—the treetops—to use. Your mind is a mental computer that takes these things into consideration. I've heard men, after their first experiences with timber shooting, express thoughts to the effect that those birds traveled faster in the woods than they ever did outside. Obviously, this isn't true; it's just that with the trees as reference points for their minds, the shooters finally had something against which to measure the mallards' deceptive speed.

Timber shooting is often most productive during very nice weather—nice from the creature-comfort point of view, not the ducking perspective. High skies, loafing birds, easy living—these are the things that can spell success in flooded woods. There are times, though, when really nasty weather will drive the birds into the woods, especially if that is the only real cover around.

Prairie hunting for puddle ducks, as practiced in the Great American Desert, is a spectacular sport. Small potholes or wide spots on rivers will produce, as will cropfields that have been picked recently.

Flooded timber shooting can be fast, especially if you're after wood ducks and other dabblers. Timber is good resting/feeding habitat and requires a minimum of equipment. Photo by Steven Griffin.

I dearly love the mechanical corn picker. Every once in a while it'll take a cob of corn and bust the thing into a zillion little pieces, each of which becomes prime feed for a duck.

Prairie shooting is the art of finding which field the birds are using to feed during the day. Typically, ducks will spend the night on a large body of water. This is their defense mechanism against predation. Come daylight and the birds will leave this sanctuary (which may, indeed, be a legal sanctuary), and fly to feed. They'll come back to water for the midday hours and then return to feed again in the afternoon before heading back to the big water and sleepy-town.

A morning hunt can be a guessing game. The birds will usually take the feed from fields closest to the water first, having to move farther and farther away each day as food decreases. Knowing where the birds fed in the morning will give you a good idea of what field to work in the afternoon.

The smart money spends time in the morning with binoculars in a car on the backcountry roads, watching for knots of birds and trying to determine flight paths and feeding fields. You can also do this in the afternoon of the day before your morning hunt. Once you've figured out which fields the birds are using, set up your decoys in a manner that looks, from the air, like dabblers feeding on the ground. The spread should feature fairly well-scattered decoys. Again, leave an open spot about where you'd like the birds to land.

I especially like dry field shooting because cripples just don't escape. Many times the fall will kill a lightly-hit bird. On one such shoot after freeze-up, I pulled a big, dark greenhead out of a flock about 35 yards up. The bird dropped, but with his head up, indicating a bird with a lot of life in him. When the Lab brought him in, stone dead, the bird's breast was split wide open. Hitting that frozen cornfield must have been like dropping into a parking lot.

Concealment in prairie shooting is often a matter of digging a pit as you would when field shooting for geese. If there are cornstalks or wheat leavings around, however, you can just lie down and cover yourself with these. Some shooters who do a lot of this kind of gunning have woven cornstalks into light chicken-wire fencing to make a blanket that they can whip off and on

again with ease. They roll it up and carry their blinds under one
arm when heading to the field.

Another appealing aspect of field shooting is the fact that
the feeding flights are rather predictable, so you can spend the
unproductive midday hours doing something else; take a nap,
go pheasant hunting, scout for new fields, it's up to you.

Once freeze-up comes to the plains, open water becomes
the key for any birds that haven't migrated through. Although
I've never tried it and therefore can't vouch for it, I've talked
with shooters who claim to have had good luck with "portable
ponds." These are merely large pieces of clear or blue plastic
that they stake out in a snowy field. Pushing snow up around
the edges to give the impression of an irregular shoreline, they
set their decoys out on the plastic. From the air, it should look
like the last open water between here and Louisiana. I'll have
to try it sometime.

Prairie shooting can also translate into field shooting in parts
of the country, aside from the Plains States, especially around
refuge areas.

As food supplies are eaten up by the birds, the farmlands
around a refuge come in for the attention of thousands of waterfowl. As a result, many of these lands bring more in lease
fees to the owners than they'd ever yield in crop income. But,
for those who can get on such lands, the principle is the same.
The birds will use certain fields morning and evening. Although
you won't have the flexibility of following the birds because of
trespass laws and so forth, you can still have good shooting if
you are aware of where the birds are likely to be.

One word of warning: the temptation to illegally bait waterfowl can run strong here, especially in the man who has several thousand dollars invested in a lease arrangement and has
limited hunting time. Remember the federal regulations regarding
such dalliances. You can leave crops standing, but you can't
introduce feed or display the feed in such a way—spreading
shelled or cobbed corn around the ground—that the intent is to
lure waterfowl into the area. This is baiting, they'll throw the
book at you, and I hope they do. Baiting is a hunting method
that takes out the ingenuity needed to identify natural food sources,
to display decoys, and to call in such a way that waterfowl are

fooled into dropping in. Baiting violates the "fair chase" ethic that all real sportsmen subscribe to.

Between the resting and feeding areas that puddle ducks use, there are sometimes places where the lay of the land or weather conditions can cause them to drop low enough so that you can get a shot at them. This is the essence of pass shooting—taking them as they pass over with no intent by you of getting them closer and no intent by them of coming down.

Many refuges have areas open for such hunting. These "firing lines" are usually well inhabited by the big-bore fraternity, and sky busting is pretty much the rule of the day. If this is the only waterfowling you have available to you, so be it. But most of my experiences with such activities have seen me come away with marks in my pipe stem from gritting my teeth.

Better pass shooting can be had from watching movements of local populations of ducks and trying to figure out how they're trading. If you've discovered that birds are using a certain pot-hole pond as a resting and loafing area during the day, for example, and if you can't set up a blind there for some reason, try to be nearby when the birds pass overhead going to or from the pond. They will usually be low enough to be within shotgun range several hundred yards from the pond, especially coming in.

Or, on the river hunts discussed earlier, you will find that ducks sometimes follow the course of the river very closely and quite low. Concealing yourself along the bank can net some shooting.

Ducks will often fly over small lakes before making their circling pass to land. At such times, any point of land jutting into the water can put you close enough to the birds so that you can get some shooting. Putting out decoys in such places will swing them by a little closer. They may have no intention of coming in, but the decoys will often swing them those last few critical yards closer so you can get a poke or two at them.

One time my pal, Mark Sutton, and I got decent shooting on the pass at mallards that were coming off a river and going to a beaver pond by flying over some sandy ridges studded with oaks. The treetops were good reference points, and since the ducks didn't have far to go and were undisturbed in that barren country, they didn't have much altitude. They were up only about 30 yards, although they looked higher because they were overhead. They filled limits for us on several gorgeous October days—the kinds of days that are lousy for more traditional forms of waterfowling.

For most puddle duck hunting, I think that a man with a good, sturdy, 14-or 16-foot canoe with a square transom for a motor will find most of his needs filled. The canoe can be used for float-tripping; it draws little water, so you can take it places where a V-bottom would hang up. The paddles make propelling it in tight situations a little easier, and the slimmer shape makes hiding it easier. They're also lightweight, which means a lot when you have to hoist it off the car at 4:00 a.m.

The main criticism of the canoe is that it's unstable when you're shooting. I've seen some pretty slick ways of getting around that. I'll outline a couple . . .

First, there are commercial outrigger attachments that you can clamp on or swing down once you're in position. These can even be put into operation if the water gets rough during your trip in or out in morning and evening.

The other method that I like, usable only in fairly shallow water, is the method employed by my pal, Charlie. He uses four poles that are about five feet long, with auger screw points on the ends. He twists these into the mud, two on each side of the canoe about one-third of the way down from the bow and the same distance from the stern. He then shoves a bar through holes in the poles opposite one another so that the canoe, in effect, is sitting underneath two very stable crossbars. He finally lashes the poles, canoe and crossbars together so that the craft doesn't drift out from underneath. Flat floorboards of marine-grade plywood painted the "OD green" of waterfowlers make the floor even, dry and easy to stand on. With this arrangement, Charlie's overweight Lab, "Jill," Charlie and I have about as stable an arrangement as you can find this side of a deepwater blind. The whole contraption can be put together in five minutes, even in the near darkness of pre-dawn. Slick.

A second, smaller canoe can be towed behind the main craft and can serve double duty. First, it's a pack mule for hauling in the decoys and other equipment you'll need; and secondly, it can be used as a secondary gunning craft for extra party members or when the spread of decoys is so large that you want a larger field of fire and it makes sense to put another guy 25 to 30 yards away.

The traditional sneakbox-type gunning boat, with the shape of a canoe and the nearly enclosed top, is also a usable craft, but really only after it's been towed into position. With no place for a motor and cramped conditions for paddling, this thing is tough to use and can be dangerous. I speak from experience. I was on Lake Huron during the November gale that sent the *Edmund Fitzgerald* to her watery grave. This freighter, with 29 men aboard, and my sneakboat had the same basic problem— we shouldn't have been out there on a day when conditions were so severe. I've come close to a lonely death in a duck boat several times. That was about the closest.

My escapades on Huron that day were made with the express intent of hunting a little bay that I knew mallards were using. And generally, when I hunt dabblers, I hunt mallards. They are, of course, the most common target for gunners across the country. Still, no chapter on dabblers would be complete without discussing some of the "specialty" species.

The first of these are the teal. Not too long ago, waterfowl biologists discovered that blue-winged teal were migrating through before the normal waterfowl seasons were underway. As a result, these birds were a resource that was "underharvested."

So, in some states, special teal seasons were set up. This is waterfowling at its most miserable, because the season usually comes in September when it's summer-hot and the bugs are still out.

Some states have seen fit to close down this season. Sadly, it may be because some hunters were treating this as a regular waterfowl season and taking pops at any duck that came close. This was never the intent, of course. But other states have had pretty good luck with the early season, and it does give hunters a chance to get out early, stretch their hunting legs and get tuned up for the "regular" season.

Teal hunting is tricky because you're after a single species, the smallest of our ducks, one that is sometimes confused with immature wood ducks. The greenwings migrate later, like more "normal" waterfowl. It's the bluewings that are the early ones.

Bluewings are more common across the Midwest and the northern tier of states, while the greenwings are a more western bird. They do overlap in the southern extent of their ranges, especially on the wintering grounds.

Teal will decoy well to mallard decoys, although you won't need nearly the number that you would if hunting the bigger birds; a couple of dozen are plenty. Using a mallard highball on the call will work, too, but there is little reason to call in many instances. Teal have a tendency to dart in low and fast, often just skimming the water, and they are less likely to make the curious passes that their bigger brothers do. If a set looks good to them, a flock of teal will just sort of clamber in. This can be disconcerting for hunters used to several passes, backpedaling and red feet over the decoys.

Hitting a teal in flight can sometimes be an all-or-nothing proposition. I can remember swinging on a flight of bluewings once, leading the first duck, and sending the dog for four dead birds that all ran into the same shot charge. I can also remember missing something like 14 straight teal once—a new outdoor record, by the way.

The other bird that could be called a specialty is the wood duck, a species which is one of the real success stories of waterfowl management.

In 1918, the numbers of this bird dropped so low that it was feared extinction was just around the corner. The drake woodie's beautiful plumage was sought for ladies' hats and other accoutrements, but it was the continuing destruction of flooded woodlands that caused the biggest problems for the birds' nesting needs. The draining of backwater sloughs to create more farmland hurt these ducks immensely, and in 1918 the season was closed on these birds nationwide and in Canada. This was actually a result of the growing awareness and management ethic that was starting to assert itself.

By 1941 the woodie had come back to the point where the season was reopened in parts of the country; and as of the early 1980s the wood duck was the most common breeding waterfowl in the eastern United States. In fact, it is now so common that it can prove frustrating to timber shooters after mallards, because once the wood duck limit is filled, the hunter may find that he is located in a woodie "honey hole" that attracts only these birds—and scores of them.

Wood duck hunting has always been, to me, more like upland hunting. The birds are likely to ignore your decoys; they might not decoy at all. If you are having woodies come into your blocks, it's probably because they wanted to be there anyway and would have come even if your stool weren't there.

The way to hunt wood ducks is to find an area where they are feeding and pursue them there. Jump shooters, in particular, are likely to encounter wood ducks, especially if their favorite river wends its way through an area vegetated predominantly by oaks. The oaks drop their acorns into the water or onto the ground near water, and the birds feed on them.

Woodies are often found quite a ways from water. I can remember jumping and shooting a drake wood duck from an open oak stand that was like a park while I was grouse hunting. There was no water within a quarter mile that I could see, yet that bird was there—and he was full of acorns. The woodie seems to get around on land quite well, thank you.

I think that part of the lure of hunting wood ducks comes from the time of year when you're most likely to get into them. Wood ducks are usually among the first ducks to migrate, normally heading out on the teeth of the first raw norther, even if the cold spell isn't prolonged. Evidently, they just like it warm and will leave if things get chilly, although I've shot them almost right up to freeze-up.

The time of year when they're around is the most beautiful of the autumn, with gorgeous colors accenting those of the duck himself. And, like upland hunting, the shooting can get tricky. Woodies will quite likely dart right in through the oak branches while you're trying to swing on them—sort of like trying to shoot a ruffed grouse. For this reason, I like an upland-type shotgun: open choked, short barrel and stocked to shoot where I'm looking. Before the days of steel shot, I did right well with a 20-gauge double shooting an ounce of No. 7½ shot. The woodie isn't a large duck, but his habitat can soak up a lot of your firepower. Today, hunting in steel shot areas—and shooting steel by choice when I'm in a lead shot zone—I do fine with No. 4 steel and a modified barrel. Most of my misses can't be traced to ballistics.

One of the best areas of the United States to hunt woodies is in the Great Plains, places such as Iowa and southern Minnesota where there are sloughs the farmers haven't gotten around to draining yet. These areas offer nesting opportunities for the birds, and the nearby fields—notably corn—provide the feed.

The birds' nesting habits—in the boles of hollow trees—have made them very popular with conservation and kids' groups. Wood duck boxes by the tens of thousands have been nailed up all across the bird's range, and I'm sure this has helped their numbers return, along with some enlightened wetlands legislation and the refuge system.

It's interesting to me that wood duck hunters, as specialists, are few in number, but if a hunter has one waterfowl mounted and in simulated flight on his den wall, it's probably an early-season adult drake wood duck, the most beautiful of all ducks.

4

The Geese

They come in and over in flocks that the average waterfowler only dreams of. They are young, mostly birds of the year. They are, frankly, quite stupid. By the time they get to Mexico, they'll be smart; right now, they're trusting. You and your partner are the first to have a go at them. You've sacrificed a lot to be here. It's the trip of a lifetime.

Hunting geese on the Canadian tundra—the treeless plain of the North, the area where the growing season is so short that only the hardiest of plants can live—is an experience that perhaps will outlive any duck hunting experience.

With the refuge system and with the nesting habitat in the sub-arctic circle, it is unlikely that the population of geese will do anything but spiral upward. Where a Canada goose was once a trophy, today he is almost a nuisance in some areas. On the tundra, you meet him at his roots.

In very few places on this earth does a man feel completely alone, totally vulnerable. The tundra is one such place. Little has changed since the last glacier receded from here, and the wind that whips off the ice pack not too many degrees north of you speaks of winter, even though you may have left September summer temperatures behind you in the States.

And the geese, if you hit it right, are there in numbers unchanged from what they must have been like when the Crees, like the man who guides you, held sway over this land and lived off the geese all winter—as he does today.

The birds nest in the regions around James Bay and Hudson's Bay proper. When the sun slants just so in the autumn sky, something in them says "go," and they begin their staging flights—not unlike World War II aircraft that marshalled from fields across England for raids on Germany.

The Bays are the last major stopovers for the birds before the flights south, and they are trading constantly across the barren reaches. Your guide knows their favorite spots, however, and so he sets out what passes for his "decoys" while you watch from a scrub-willow blind. The decoys may be chunks of tundra mud with sticks protruding, old rags or even newspapers. Quality, here, counts for little; it's a numbers game.

Your shooting will primarily be at flocks consisting of four to ten birds, family groups, mainly, and the liberal five-bird limit is quite a load to carry back to camp. Once that limit is filled, there are other chances for sport: pass shooting at ducks, sharptail or ptarmigan hunting, fishing for brook trout or even hunting snipe, a sport of generations ago.

Back at "camp," which is actually a lodge that can feature either plush or Spartan accommodations, depending on how much you want to spend, you'll sit around sipping red pops and trading lies with the other parties, all of whom have probably returned by midafternoon. You'll find that there are few repeat hunters in this group. This doesn't speak poorly of your outfitter, though. Instead, most of the goose hunters will be like you: first-timers from the States who have saved their nickels and dimes to finance this trip after years of waiting in line for a public blind in a public marsh for a chance at shooting a well-educated public goose.

During your hunt, you'll notice a strange metamorphosis taking place. Easy shots on decoying birds will be passed up in favor of the tough-angle bird; young, unmated, tender birds will be chosen over adults; a bird will be sought that will make a "mounter" for a den or office; flocks will be called in and no shots taken, the satisfaction coming from hearing the sub-arctic wind whispering through primaries; you'll try to take a mixed bag of snows, blues and maybe three subspecies of Canadas. Many of the Canadas were hatched on the shores of Hudson's

A field shoot for geese is usually a matter of setting up before dawn in a field you know— or guess—the birds will be using. Photo by Steven Griffin.

Bay. The snows and blues were fledged farther north, but they migrate through the bay in spring and fall.

In fact, this is what makes the bay what it is: The Atlantic and Mississippi flyways do not separate until farther south, so geese that will use one flyway or the other are all found in Hudson's Bay and James Bay during the fall. Here they will fatten, grow stronger after the rigors of nesting (and growing up), and wait for the synergistic signal to head south.

Your equipment will be simple and functional: probably personal belongings for camp, perhaps a sleeping bag, hip boots, camo clothing (plan for foul weather), some down clothing (the weather can be anything from sleet storms to 80°F. in September), a pair of 12-gauge guns (who wants a broken firing pin on your only gun that far from home?) and some shells. By the way, you're a lot better off buying shells in Canada after you've arrived than trying to ship them through customs and on the airlines. Most air carriers have apoplexy when you present a cased, broken-down gun: they have a hemorrhage when you tell them you've got the ammunition, too.

For most of us, shooting geese on the tundra is a dream that will probably never be lived.

But the dream of waterfowl managers to bring back the Canada goose is a reality. This bird has become a symbol of the progress made through proper management and is a scientific success story. The Canada—and there are several species—is probably our most recognizable goose. Incorrectly referred to as "Canadian" geese, these birds and their Vs in the sky are a herald of autumn and spring as they pass overhead.

When they pass overhead, they are probably headed for a publicly-managed hunting/refuge area, and herein lies the tale. The refuge system has given these great birds a place to call home on the way to and from the wintering grounds to the south and the sub-arctic nesting grounds.

Most refuges host a "native population." These are birds that have simply said, "To hell with all this flapping around. I like it here and I'm going to stay." And stay they do. The resident populations of birds that winter over at some refuges number many thousands, but those that pass through coming and going swell that number tenfold.

In most such areas, a quota system has been set for how many geese can safely be taken by gunners every season, and when that quota is met, the season is closed for that spot. The limits and hunting hours vary, but in most places the quotas and limits have continued to rise. To give you an example, there was a time on one managed area that I hunt that one goose a season was all that was allowed. Now it's two a day in the mornings, and you don't have to be in a special goose hunting area as in the old days. Now we can shoot a pair of geese every day, mornings only.

Strangely, when you're hunting ducks in the afternoon and geese aren't the quarry, these big birds can actually get in the way. A single or a pair will drone right in like bombers, not making a pass or a look-over, but just sailing in. Last season three geese decided to come in to our blocks at the same time that four mallards were making their final pass. The geese cluttered up the area and made shooting at the ducks impossible because we were afraid of taking an illegal goose by mistake—it was in the afternoon and goose shooting was closed for the day. These birds acted as if they could practically tell time; either that or they were incredibly stupid for a species that had been hunted half days for a month. More than likely they were young birds down from the north only recently.

The young birds, as in Canada, make up the majority of those geese brought to bag. Typically, early in the season, a family group—ma, pa and five or six young' uns—is what most shooters get action on. The youngsters are the ones most likely to come into a set while the old-timers hang off and out of range. But as the shooting progresses, geese smarten up in a hurry.

As far as innate intelligence is concerned, the Canadas of the various subspecies lead. With seven-power eyesight, extreme wariness most of the time and wisdom born of a long lifespan, an old Canada gander is the waterfowl equivalent of a 12-point buck with a Roman nose; he didn't get that way by being stupid. The rest of the geese, blues, snows and whitefronts, rank somewhere below Canadas.

Snows, in my opinion, are not as bright as mallards, and are nowhere near a gun-smart black duck. When they are present in good numbers and working fields, it's no great trick to take a limit of these birds. The various subspecies of brant are even further down the scale, and their decline in numbers can be blamed on this to some degree, along with bad weather on breeding grounds and, in some cases, unlimited hunting by native Americans guaranteed by law under ancient treaties.

Hunting geese in the United States today is mostly a matter, as indicated earlier, of hunting the areas around refuges. Although each refuge along the major flyways has areas open to hunting, most of the geese taken are probably taken on private land bordering the refuges. These lands, and the methods used to hunt them, are directly linked to the refuges. I'll bet that for every five geese shot this past season in the United States, three of them woke up the day they died within the sanctuary of a refuge.

Goose shooting is, today, typically a field-shooting affair, or it's pass shooting. Let's take a look.

Not too long ago both geese and hunters of geese did their thing on water, like ducks and duck hunters. But, these birds quickly adapted to the ways of the mechanical harvesting machine. Like ducks on the prairies, they have become grazers and feeders on waste grain left behind by the picking machines. Pass shooting and field shooting are closely related to one another. Here's how . . .

The sun comes up. Being somewhat of a lazy gent, the goose doesn't get up with the chickens. He will usually wait an hour or two until things warm up a bit. The birds start talking to each other, and the din before liftoff can be deafening—partly from the sound of adrenaline-surged blood being pumped through your ear canals.

The birds rise in great waves off the refuge, circle upward to a hundred yards or so, and then pass over the boundaries of the refuge on their way to the outlying fields to feed. By the time the season is open even a week, the birds have probably cleaned out the feed in the refuge and must go off-site to fill up. It is when they fly over the "firing line" that they can be vulnerable to the pass shooter.

A number of factors can make the geese pass low over the firing line, and these will be discussed in the chapter on weather patterns. Suffice it to say right now that miserable weather makes the birds stay closer to earth and puts them in range of the guns.

The birds that survive the pass over the firing line—probably most of them—make their way to the fields to feed. The birds start with the fields closest to the refuge, naturally, and gradually move farther and farther away as feed in these nearby fields is exhausted. Getting onto such fields to hunt is usually a matter of coin of the realm, as the owners of the land have come to regard waterfowl as a well-paying cash crop. Junior can go to Harvard with the money Pop gets from leasing his prime fields.

The birds drop in to the areas to feed, and it is here that some skill is required. Getting a blind prepared for goose hunting is much like the espionage business; it's carried on under cover of darkness, or at least when the enemy isn't looking. The pit blind—an actual hole in the ground—is the most common arrangement. With natural cover such as cornstalks to shield you, and a good spread of decoys, you're probably in business if the birds want to use your field. Setting up in a field that the birds have cleaned out does little good; they know before they even leave the refuge that your field is like the cupboard of the good widow Hubbard, and will pass you by. Scouting the afternoon

Geese, being primarily grazers, often tempt hunters into trying for some impromptu "stalk and rush" shooting. But, a flock such as this will always have a few sentinels on guard. Photo by Joe Workosky.

flight the day before will tell you where the birds are heading, but that won't do you any good unless you have a way to get onto the place they're headed.

The dirt taken from the pit blind should either be hidden in some manner or carted off. Leaving a hole with surrounding debris must look from the air like the result of incoming artillery fire, and affects the birds about the same way.

A compromise is a small pit into which you can dangle your feet while you sit on the edge. Such a "foot pit" works out okay if you have sufficient cover to hide the rest of you. About all it does is get you a little lower into the earth.

The decoys you haul out for geese, especially if you've had the chance to hunt with a guide or on a commercial spread, are staggering in number. I'd say that a good spread would number several hundred. Down in the southern reaches of the United States, where snow goose shooting is a big-time operation, the accepted practice is to scatter white rags on stubble in such a manner so that the cloth looks like a flock of feeding geese; even newspaper, if there is no wind, is suitable. A thousand such lures makes an effective, easy-to-carry rig. But then, snow geese aren't Canadas when it comes to brains.

Old tires have also been used, the tire being cut so the curved portion resembles the body of a goose, with a stick added for the head.

Still, the hollow-body or silhouette decoy is by far the best for geese. Always position a few with heads up. Geese have very well-developed flock (gaggle?) dynamics, and part of the defense mechanism they have is the fact that there are almost always two or three birds with their heads bolt upright and watching while the rest feed. Any spread that has all the heads down will alarm these birds because, as someone probably once said, "It ain't nat'chul."

Geese coming into the decoys have a peculiar glide pattern that is both exciting and at times heart-stopping. Sometimes they'll make up their collective mind to drop in from a great altitude. This gives them time to give things a look-see. With their wings set, heads craned, they stop all forward movement and begin that peculiar "waffling" downward, dropping many feet per second. This quickly brings them into range, and birds that looked a long way off are suddenly just *there*. Once they are beyond a certain point in their commitment, it's too late for them to reverse the drop and fight their way up again. But, they are masters at sideslipping. This waffling is so dramatic that I've seen birds almost turn over to slip air off their wings. At the last second, they backpedal and lightly set down. Amazing—and thrilling.

Low-flying birds will sometimes get the jump on goose hunters who have their necks craned to the skies. Usually, the birds will make their pass low—say, 20 yards up—in stiff wind conditions. At such times the hunter screams something intelligent like, "Ohmuhgawd!" and starts blazing away at the flock.

Instead, the proper way to handle the situation is this: The birds are low because they're fighting the wind. The wind brings them down in altitude because, normally, they're looking for a place to set down, and the wind is a little less intense down there anyway.

As the flock hoves into view, or into range, the birds should be taken when the *last,* not the first, members of the group are in range. The reason for this is because once you start shooting, the birds will do the natural thing and try to escape. To do this quickly, they must go *with* the wind. This brings them back across in front of you, even the leaders. If you shoot when only the leaders are in range, the whole flock will turn back and you'll only get chances at the forward guard. Slick. Now, just try not to lose it when those huge *maximas* are right on the end of your gun barrel. Also, remember the guy next to you hollering "Ohmuhgawd!" and blazing away is probably me. I give advice better than I take it.

Unlike many forms of waterfowling, calling is very important in goose hunting. There are four basic "honks," and variations on these. The gregarious nature of geese makes it easy to talk with them and seduce them with a call.

The Indians of Canada do a pretty fair job with their voices although, in truth, they are talking to some pretty immature— spell that naive—geese most of the time. I always get the impression that geese are surprised that anything on the ground that looks like a goose and sounds like a goose couldn't be a goose, but that's probably just me.

One of the best ways to call is with a *good* call. Most of the big-barreled commercially-marketed calls are true-toned enough to be passable. The ticket is to use it. When you see a flock of geese, cut loose at them. You'll rarely ruin the quality of the calling with volume, so don't be bashful. Once you have the birds coming your way, slow it down, muffle it or stop altogether, especially if you see that they have their wings set. Just be ready.

Canadas are the toughest to fool, brant the easiest, and the rest of the geese are somewhere in between—a function of intelligence as indicated earlier.

There are times when everything I've said about calling geese, goose pits, goose decoys and the rest is rendered void. That's when you get the chance for "The Ambush." This little foray into the Realm of the Ill-Conceived Plot takes place when you think you can get close enough to a flock of grazing geese to make an all-out, wader-flopping, eye-bulging, Pickett-at-Gettysburg charge which, you have deduced, will put you into range of the big birds before they know what's happening.

But, the scenario continues. Once you are close enough, you and perhaps a partner will screech to a halt, and each of you will neatly fold a pair of fat honkers from the melee of wings and craning necks, saving your third shell as a reserve against

A goose hunter and his dog pick up their decoys at the end of a day. Often, the best action in goose and duck hunting comes in those last few precious seconds of sunlight. Photo by Joe Workosky.

the chance—however unlikely—that one of the birds should need the *coup de grace.*

I've tried this scheme a couple of times, and Friend, it ain't easy. The first problem comes with finding a flock, but that can eventually be done. The most reachable of the birds is still likely to be several hundred yards away when you start your stalk. What you need is a handy drainage ditch, streambed or some other cover to hide you while you stalk the birds.

By now you've probably gathered that I haven't been blessed with too many successful experiences using The Ambush. How perceptive of you. Well, hunting is supposed to be recreation—fun. Anything we can do to spice things up ought to be looked at, anyway.

So you've found your streambed and your cooperative gaggle of feeding honkers. And you've stalked along the bed until you're pretty sure that you're in range of the birds—or at least as close as you're going to get. Now you and Pard leap out of the ditch and charge the geese. Right off, you'll discover that you're about three times as far away from the birds as you thought, which is about six times as far away from them as you'd hoped. You also notice (you're perceptive, remember?) that the distance is increasing in a hurry because the birds are in various stages of flight and picking up speed. If you are a slob, you'll shoot anyway and probably cripple a bird or two. If you're a real waterfowler, you'll stop your mad dash, swear reverently and colorfully, spit, grin at your partner, and head for the car. So much for The Ambush.

For those who can't tolerate the firing line near the refuges, or whose Aunt Hortence is still gulping air and her will is, as yet, unread and so the goose club is out of the question, what can you do to get in some shooting? What are the chances of prospecting for geese? Well, the chances are there, but they're slim.

During early autumn, especially in the northern tier of states, geese are starting to flock up. Along about the time the season opens, this flocking may or may not have been completed. We're talking, now, about birds that have nested in the States rather than in Canada. Small ponds, small lakes and backwater areas that harbored a nesting pair of birds throughout the spring and summer are potential hunting spots during the fall. Check them out—with permission, of course.

Backwater areas such as the kind you would look for while jump shooting ducks can also produce geese on occasion. But for the most part, any birds taken this way are bonuses. The exception to this can sometimes be a blind on a big river. Here, the large birds seem to like to congregate and feed out of the swift current. The downstream sides of islands are especially good, and a mixed bag of ducks and geese from island shooting is a rule in many parts of the country.

I like to think that the day will come when I have enough cash to walk right out and plunk down a couple of grand for a membership in an exclusive goose hunting club, one of those near a refuge with the best fields, the finest blinds, guides who actually speak the language of both goose and human and a nice clubhouse stocked with Virginia Gentleman and bitters. Such a place would have a large fireplace that I can lean against so I'll have something to warm me while I tell the lies I made up about my shooting.

Shooting leases for such lands run high; my "couple grand" estimate is probably laughable, really, for such a club.

But such goose clubs do exist, and some have many members who pay less, shoot less, but still have more hunting opportunities for geese than they could otherwise enjoy. I think that waterfowl clubs are important enough that I'm devoting a chapter of this book to them. So, as they say, "stay tuned" for more on this count.

I don't know about you, but I suspect you're like me; you like to watch waterfowl all year long, and not just during the gunning season. Each spring, the waterfowl come back from the South in hordes.

When the geese return, it's a harbinger of spring. Many folks don't realize that these regal birds actually return to a given area in the spring much earlier than usually thought, slipping in under cover of darkness. There's an 80-acre field near my home which is usually planted to beans or corn. It's hard against a river, and each spring the runoff from melting snow floods that field. The waste grain left from last autumn's harvest, coupled with the water, tempts ducks—and especially geese—in. They come overhead in almost unbelievable numbers as the sun lowers. They give quite a show to the several hundred people who drive out each evening to watch.

The birds seem oblivious to the people below: shouting kids, adults laughing and pointing, the odd Lab barking out of sheer frustration. They just keep pitching in, wave after wave, until several thousand are there.

As they come, they honk at each other constantly. I think they're talking about the places where they've been and the places they're going to, where no trees grow and where no man walks. They're singing the old song, as ancient as the sound of wind sifting through primary flight feathers, as old as the earth. I like that song. With geese, it's a song that promises to be here as long as man is here.

Maybe longer.

5

The Weather

As I start to write this, I am surrounded by a ream of data. This data covers the last several years and gives the day-to-day, hour-by-hour weather changes that have taken place from a large class-A recording weather station very near a large wildlife refuge.

This stuff, which I got from the U.S. Climatological boys, is accompanied by the kill data from that refuge, data which shows when hunter success was the greatest in terms of numbers of ducks and geese taken per hunter hour, what the species were, and which areas of the refuge produced the best. This refuge offers hunting in flooded woods, flooded cropfields, rivers, potholes and less-than-flooded areas called "moist soil units."

Also, as I write this, I am trying to thaw out from a day I

59

spent in a blind with my friends Charlie Lichon and Dave Oeming. Oeming's a lawyer, which means that Charlie and I kept alert by baiting him with our opinions of the sad state of jurisprudence as it exists today, but that's neither here nor there. What *is* here and there is the fact that we started the day with a gentle breeze and temps in the 50s. By the time late afternoon rolled around, the wind was blowing rain and sleet horizontally because the temperatures had plunged below freezing. We expected great things from the ducks. What we got was wet. Plus, we ran out of cutting remarks about Oeming.

Charlie and Dave predicted a banner shoot the next day. Since they are more or less gainfully employed, they could hunt. Being an outdoor editor, I had to work and couldn't make it. A blizzard blew up that night; we had been on the edge of the front which produced that weather condition. The next day Charlie, Dave and another lad shot two geese each (the legal limit), three ducks each, and were done by 11 in the morning.

Strange that the birds hadn't moved down on that front when I was there waiting for them. Outside of the fabled Smith Luck, there was no reason for it. But then again, there was.

The ducks, big red-legged "northern birds," mainly mallards, hadn't moved down yet, and they didn't when that front blew up. Instead, they moved down in the wee hours of the morning, perhaps the night before, pushed along by the first major cold snap of the year, and a snap that was prolonged. Herein, as they say, hangs the tale.

Some work with the previously-alluded-to data indicates some things that can be of help to the average waterfowler. First off, day-to-day weather changes can make ducks and geese edgy, but otherwise not much happens to them. A chilly night with some rain, and not much happens. Rather, it is the prolonged periods of inclement weather—rain/snow, falling temperatures, plunging barometers, winds from a northern quadrant and overcast skies—that trigger the main migrations which are the boon of the waterfowler.

During the duck season, you have probably had fine shoots during good weather and lousy hunts when all the conditions looked right. Most hunters have come to associate good duck weather with your life hanging in the balance, good waterfowling weather being the type when you could die out there. And, for the most part, this is true.

Light snow is good weather to hunt in; so is fog. The birds are less wary and their eyesight, sharp as it is, is rendered somewhat less than effective. They will decoy more readily in such conditions, too. Light rain or drizzle is also good, probably for the same reason. Heavy rain or a real blizzard isn't so great, but the hours just *before* a heavy rain or when a blizzard is in the making can be fantastic, as ducks feed heavily and look for a place to hole up.

Overcast skies can make ducks and geese want to feed more actively during daylight hours. Overcast skies prevent them from feeding at night because of reduced visibility, so they have to feed during the day. Also, the low-pressure air associated with overcast conditions probably makes flying more difficult, saps strength and increases the need for food intake. Maybe only the ducks know for sure, and they aren't talking.

Still, there are conditions around which the hunter can plan his outings and have somewhat of an advantage. First, we have to understand the givens of waterfowl migration.

Waterfowl migrate, essentially, from north to south. There are wide variations east and west, but eventually, and except for the native flocks on refuges, the birds leave the northern latitudes and head south.

There is a synergism of factors which prompts this migration: the shortening daylight hours cause a hormonal change that triggers the migration urge. Without this triggering, all migratory fowl would have died out long ago as winter closed in on their food supply and starvation took over.

The migratory urge, then, is directly food-related. Beasts such as ducks and geese, being primarily water-oriented, would find their food supply locked in by cold and, with the typically fast metabolism of all birds—a function of keeping their body weight light for flight—starvation would come quickly. So, the little buggers migrate.

Now, not all weather conditions make the birds pack up and head south. Certainly there are times when mild, short-lived weather changes merely make them more active, but these changes, too, increase the hunter's chances of doing well.

From what I've been able to determine, the changes that make for good shooting are of the type that are going to be around for a while.

For example, I found that a wind from the northern quadrants coupled with a falling thermometer *and* a drop in air pressure made waterfowl very active *just as these conditions started to take place.*

In other words, the activity of a major front moving through from the northwest, north or northeast seems to get the birds going. If the front is accompanied by some precipitation—rain, sleet, snow—so much the better. Evidently, the dropping barometer makes flight more difficult for the birds, and so they do their feeding while they still can—before the drop in air pressure has reached the point where they expend too much energy flying.

It is the intent of ducks and geese, I think, to not become the victims of bad weather conditions, so therefore they do one of two things before such a front moves in: They either migrate before it, or they actively feed and then stay put, basically, for the duration of the front.

The data I looked over, for example, showed that when a three-to-five-day blow moved in—with snow or rain, falling temperatures and air pressure, and northerly winds—the birds were very active in the morning if the front came in during the afternoon, or were active in the afternoon if the front arrived that evening. The weather data I used showed the hour-by-hour weather changes, so I was able to pinpoint when the front blew in.

Thus, if you are trying to plan your hunts for time and place, I'd suggest that you read the newspaper weather maps and make sure that you are hunting on the day—within a few hours, if possible—when a new weather front is moving in. The best hunting will be within hours of that front's arrival. If the weather pattern stays for a few days, waterfowl activity will fall right off for the duration of the pattern.

As the front moves out and fair weather returns, however, the birds will become active again. This is probably due to the fact that they have been sitting around waiting for the bad weather to leave and for high-pressure air to return, and thus make flight easier. Flight takes energy, and energy requires food. During bad weather, birds are more apt to sit tight and wait until easier flight conditions, all of this a function of conserving energy. After the fair weather returns, they are hungry from the wait and will start actively feeding again.

Most of the activity associated with these in-and-out fronts takes place in waterfowl feeding areas. If you are in a place where they will go to wait out bad weather, such as in flooded woods or a river's backwaters, then your action will take place just *as* the front moves in. By then, the birds will have filled up and will be looking for a place to wait it out.

But if you are hunting the grainfields and flooded crop-fields—where food is the primary draw—then just before the front moves in and just as the front moves out are the prime times to hunt.

Setting up on the northernmost limits of a managed area with a large spread of decoys can convince the "northerns" that they should set down there after their arduous flight. Your spread is the first they'll see after hours of flying.

The times when low-pressure air hangs over your digs, and ducks and geese aren't on the move, are when you should do some prospecting. Now is when you should be checking out the backwater sloughs, canals, wilderness rivers and the like. It is in these places that the ducks will hang out, essentially finding the places that can give them food, a modicum of protection from the elements and safety.

The nights of the full moon, for those of us who hunt geese, are also bad times to be hunting the next day. As the shooting season progresses, the majestic birds start playing dirty: They start feeding at night when skies are clear. This presents all sorts of problems for goose hunters, as night hunting is not only hard as hell, it's also illegal.

So, some of the best times to go after geese are during the days immediately following overcast nights or when there is no moon. Traditionally, the days following clear nights of the harvest moon are a bust; at least, they have been for me.

During wind-swept days on big water, ducks are looking to raft up on the lee side of some projection such as a point of land. Be sure that your decoy setup takes on the natural appearance of waterfowl at rest. That is, make sure that you set up on the downwind side of such a point of land or in some cove, bay or harbor where waterfowl would naturally come to relax when things got choppy.

If divers are your fare, watch as a November blow enters its second day. Many times, bluebills won't move off from the safety of big water until the wind has had a chance to work them over for 24 hours or so. After they get it through what passes for their minds that the wind isn't likely to stop for a while, they are more likely to start splitting off in pairs and small flocks from the main body and heading along shorelines looking for shelter. Be there.

6

The Dogs

Although this will probably turn quite a few people into former readers, I might as well get it right out in front: Anyone who hunts waterfowl without a dog should be suspended over a slow fire for an unspecified period of time.

There, I've said it and I'm glad. Unlike in some other bird hunting sports, a good dog in waterfowling is more than just a pleasure, great though that pleasure is. A good, well-trained dog is a conservation agent of the first order, and is probably a more valuable piece of equipment than a bag of decoys.

Alas, cripples are a fact of life in waterfowling. Marginal shots are taken too many times, and ducks and geese are tenacious of life unlike their more fragile upland brethren. In addition, the diving and swimming tendencies of wounded fowl are legendary. All of these things conspire to make a shameful birdshit vs. birds-brought-to-bag ratio. What can be done to improve the situation? A good dog.

Several breeds leap to mind as effective duck dogs. The Labrador retriever is probably the best known because of a variety of traits, all of them good. First, Labs are so damned smart it's almost scary. Secondly, they are of a winsome temperament in the home, making them welcome companions. Thirdly, they have the heart of a lion in all but the most discouraging conditions. Their intelligence also makes this breed easy to train, but more on training later.

For those who like a more rugged dog, and who hunt in especially rugged conditions, the Chesapeake Bay retriever is tough to beat. These dogs run toward more weight than a Lab, and were the dog of choice among many market gunners. Legend has it that the Chessie could not only break ice to retrieve his master's bag in the worst weather, but also did guard duty over the decoys, guns, boats and assorted minutiae when master trundled his ducks off to market.

The Chessie has come under some bad press due to his independence, but many of the problems result when a mature dog is sold or given away to a new owner. The Chessie is a one-man dog, and using harsh methods on him only brings out his worst side. The breed doesn't have quite the adaptability of the Lab if you plan to use your retriever for upland hunting as well, and the Lab is better with children and other small humans. But, for the man who wants a pure retriever, the Chessie will give service day after day in weather that would rebuff the Ostrogoths.

If it's kindness and a gentle nature you want, and you're an even-handed, gentle trainer, it would be hard to beat the beautiful golden retriever. This breed is among the "softest" of the sporting dogs, the opposite of the Chessie.

Intelligent and loving, the golden is a fine water dog and can serve double duty in the uplands. I think this breed is among the smartest of all dogs, but it can have problems when pro trainers try to use "efficient" training methods. The golden will just not stand up under heavy-handed training, and a trainer can ruin a dog if he's not careful. Maybe that's why the Lab is so popular:

Get heavy-handed with a golden, and he sulks; get heavy-handed with a Chessie, and you'd do well to start counting your fingers. A Lab can handle it without losing his fire or rebelling.

More and more, waterfowlers are starting to go to the more exotic, versatile breeds such as the puddlepointer, German wirehaired pointer, the griffon and other continental breeds. Among these, I'd have to give the wirehair the nod as being the best of the lot if you do some upland gunning and a lot of waterfowling. The coat is protective, the nose on the breed is exceptional, they are companionable, and the retrieving instinct is strongly developed. My guess is that it won't be long before this breed starts

Even an experienced dog needs between-seasons tuning up. Here, the basics are reinforced in an old campaigner prior to the season. Photo by Steven Griffin.

displacing some of the more popular specialty breeds, because of its ability to handle all jobs—even trailing—so well.

Other breeds deserve mention, with the American water spaniel, the Irish water spaniel and the giant poodle—a real rarity—among them.

But day in and day out, it's still the Lab you see waiting with his master for the sun to come up, supervising the decoy operations, trying to eat your lunch when you're not looking, and smacking his human pal's frozen lips with a wet tail—all the things dogs do so well in the confines of a duck blind.

The dog's purpose, as stated earlier, goes beyond the companionship of having someone to talk to when the ducks aren't moving; the retriever is a real conservation agent. No, put it this way: A *well-trained* retriever is a real conservation agent.

The training of a dog should begin young; six to seven weeks isn't too early to let the animal become acquainted with his name, expose him to loud noises that will stop gunshyness or gun nervousness later on. The basic function of a retriever is to get ducks that you see go down, and to find ducks that neither of you know the exact location of. To do this, the man-dog relationship has to be a real partnership. The dog should be trained to—and be willing to—take direction from the handler, and the handler should allow the dog to use his instincts and senses when that's the better part of valor.

The basic commands that any retriever should know are: "Sit," "Stay" and "Come." In addition, there are the other nuances of taking a line, getting "back" and responding to whistle commands. You want the dog to be able to go where he's directed, whether he is right in front of you or 200 yards out in a driving gale.

The reason for "sit," of course, is that this is what you want the dog to do in the blind and also because it is from the sitting position that the dog will be sent after his line is given to him. "Stay" means just that, as does "Come." Upon a whistle signal, the dog should face you, sitting, and wait for the direction, given with the arms and perhaps another whistle signal, in which you want him to search.

"Taking a line" is when you send the dog in a particular direction toward a duck or goose that he hasn't seen come down.

Fewer sights are more likely to gladden the heart of a Lab man than a black dog hitting the water. The Lab is the most popular of the retriever species, and with good reason—the breed is strong, affectionate, easily trainable, and so smart it's scary. Photo by Steven Griffin.

He has to trust that there will be something there for him to find, so all training should emphasize the fact that there is a reward at the end of the line you've given him.

One way to keep a young dog on line during training is to do so in a grassy field in which paths have been mowed, and with a boat bumper or retriever dummy on the path somewhere. You have the dog sit next to you, give him the line by pointing alongside his head, motioning the direction, then release him. He will, naturally, run along the mowed trail until he hits the dummy. A "Come" will bring both dog and bumper back to you.

Teaching a dog to "get back" or "over" is also accomplished through extensive and intensive yard training. Using a baseball-diamond type of setup, you place the pup on the pitcher's mound with yourself at home plate. Then, using arm motions and exaggerated body motions, you point in the direction you want the dog to move. Mowing paths in a field to first, second and third bases will speed him along, in the beginning, toward the destinations you have in mind.

There are a number of top-notch training books on the market that carry the instructions for specifically training retrievers. I'd suggest *Gun Dog Training Spaniels and Retrievers,* by Ken Roebuck, a good friend, and *Water Dog,* a classic in the field by another friend, Richard A. Wolters.

Keeping a dog in trim means working him every chance you get. After work, 15 minutes a day, is better than spending half a day on Saturday with him, and it's best to step up the training sessions once the season draws closer. Using a firing dummy launcher, make sure that the dog gets enough water work. Chasing down a crippled but lively mallard in a gale in four-foot-deep water is no place for a dog that's out of shape.

Thinking of the little things can make the trips for waterfowl more enjoyable. For example, teaching a dog to shake after a retrieve *outside* the blind is a good way to make points with hunting buddies and also a good way to forestall pneumonia. It's also a good idea, wherever possible, to have a raised platform for the dog to sit on while in the boat or blind. From this platform, your dog can mark the falls of shot ducks and also stay dry and comfortable during the hunt. He'll perform better as a result.

The retriever network in this country is well-oiled and runs

A well-trained retriever is the best conservation agent there is. In areas where dogs are used regularly, the number of cripples that go unrecovered has dropped dramatically. Photo by Steven Griffin.

smoothly, several good periodicals are put out by knowledgeable people concerning the retrieving breeds, and field trialing among these so afflicted reaches a fervor.

Fortunately, there is some sense for the hunter. A fairly new organization, the *North American Hunting Retriever Association,* founded, among others, by the aforementioned Dick Wolters, promises good things in the years to come by providing a forum for exhibition of real hunting skills and ranking of real hunting retrievers—and not just those dogs that many feel are machines bred and trained to perform impossible field-trial feats against impossible odds and situations.

Gene Hill once told me that he had a fine Persian rug in his home that had a hole in it through which a medium-sized half-track could be driven, thanks to the gastronomical gymnastics of his Labs, Sarah and Maggie. He also remarked that this matched the sofa and a couple of chairs, which were also munched upon. He sort of sighed and looked off into the distance as he was telling me this.

This is the best tribute I've ever heard to a dog: a sigh that says he wouldn't change anything. He just wished he'd had a chance to cover it up before his wife found out.

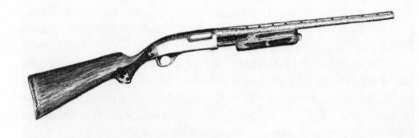

7

The Guns

Waterfowl guns have traditionally been looked upon as long-barreled, big-gauge pieces that will give that "smooth swing" which ensures enough lead.

But, the hunting conditions and the art of shooting a duck or goose vary so greatly that waterfowl guns are actually specialty items. In the broader sense, there probably isn't an ideal all-round shotgun anymore—and there probably never was. Instead, the smart waterfowler will fit his gun and load to the conditions existing at the place and time that he hunts. Further complicating matters are steel-shot restrictions that are and/or probably will become facts of life for waterfowlers as the 21st century approaches.

In the matter of actions, there are three basic types: the

73

double, either over/under or side-by-side, the pump and the autoloader. With steel shot as a factor, many shooters choose to stay away from the doubles, fearing damage to the walls of the barrels of a fine double. This is probably smart. A well-constructed double usually has very thin barrels that could be bulged by the extra-hard steel, which won't deform and "give" as it passes through the chokes of such a gun. Some hunters use doubles with impunity. I leave mine home.

The autoloader has long since reached a degree of reliability that makes it a fine choice for the waterfowler. Among these, the Remington Model 1100 in the gas-operated shotguns is hard to beat, and the recoil-operated, hump-backed Browning has probably splashed more ducks than almost any other.

The auto offers some advantages, too. First, with the federal three-shot limit, it offers the extra firepower needed when a bird drops with its head up and a follow-up shot must be taken quickly. The auto also makes shooting easier because the hunter, normally bundled up like a Siberian border guard, has fewer physical gyrations to go through to get off that second and then third shot. Felt recoil is less too.

On the other hand, this model has some drawbacks as well. It is usually heavier than either the double or pump, and the balance is normally a little less fine. A gun can be made to balance well by the addition of weight, but who wants to carry a heavier gun? Not me! And, once an auto breaks on you in the marsh, you are usually out of commission. Being of a complex manufacture, the auto has more things that can go wrong with it—some of them terminal.

The pump gun is a good compromise between the handling of a double and the firepower of an autoloader. It runs a bit lighter, holds three shots and balances a bit better. The felt recoil, like the fixed-breech doubles, is greater, and it takes a little longer to crack off three rounds, but that can benefit the shooter by making him concentrate between shots and slowing him down so he's more effective. The average gunner finds that there's an awful lot of sky around each duck, and filling that space with shot doesn't do anybody any good—well, maybe the duck.

The pump is also a little more foolproof than the auto. It costs less, too, a factor to be considered when the end of the season rolls around and you take a good look at your pet goose stopper. Strange things can happen to the finish of a good gun while it's inside a good duck boat, and none of them are very good.

Pump guns by the major manufacturers also offer rather inexpensive options such as extra barrels, which can give your battery the versatility it needs to cope with the varying situations that duck and goose hunters can encounter in a season. In some cases, it would be wise to have several guns of the same make with varying barrel lengths, stock dimensions, chokes and recoil-reducing apparatuses.

The pump also comes into action quicker when birds are spooky and just won't come in. At such times I've wished I had my five-and-a-half-pound woodcock gun instead of my pet fowling piece, as the speed of mounting would give me a chance at those birds yards closer, before they really got serious about flaring off.

Among the pumps, the Winchester Model 12 is considered the "perfect repeater," but getting harder to come by on the used-gun market. The Remington 870 has been a standard for years, while the Ithaca 37 is a favorite of mine if I think I'll be doing some jump shooting, when speed of handling and lighter carrying weight have to be considered. As far as recoil in a light duck gun, sorry—I only feel recoil when I'm pattern testing.

I haven't mentioned gauge so far, so now I will: 12. I'm a real advocate of fast-handling shotguns in small gauge for most hunting. I hunt grouse and woodcock with 20s or my smooth old five-and-three-quarter-pound Parker 16-gauge; but for waterfowl, I want the power that only a 12 can give me. In some areas, 10-gauge guns are allowed, and the Ithaca Mag-10 is the best choice of these, but I feel that you don't need a Roman candle shell if your decoying, calling and site selection are what they should be. Maybe the 10 would fit in some pass shooting situations, but otherwise a good 12-gauge load of one-and-one quarter ounces of lead—one-and-one-eighth ounces of steel—is about all you'll need. The market hunters rarely used more than an ounce of shot from their 10-gauge guns and made a living at it.

Before we get into the aspects of loads and chokes for waterfowling, let's talk a bit about the type of shooting conditions and what it takes to kill a duck or goose related to the typical—if there are such things—shooting conditions.

Diver duck shooting is normally a cold-weather affair. The birds really carry it, and they normally don't throw you a knuckleball when it comes time to start firing. Divers will normally just pour it on and keep going, often passing very near the blind or sneakboat even though the guns are blazing.

Because of this, and because multiple kills are possible, a repeating shotgun is best. Cold weather saps the strength of a shotshell, and the wind often associated with diver shooting can put a real bow in your shot string, sometimes moving it several feet at 40 yards, which is the maximum, sure killing range of a good 12-gauge load with the proper choke.

So, divers take a lot of killing. They are typically well-feathered and fat when they move down from the north for their migration flights, and this also means they need to be hit hard with a good load of shot.

When you get strafed by a formation of divers, the men in the blind should make sure that they understand the nuances of shooting at such a flock. The man closer to the front of the flock—the person on the right, if the birds approach from the right—should work on the birds at the end of the flock; his partner should take the leaders. This is a good technique regardless of the species of birds, even dabblers, because it ensures that both men will have shooting. Ducks more likely to flare, such as wary mallards, will back off when the guns start to crack, and unless the lead man lets the lead ducks get in where his partner can shoot, only the front ducks will get attention and then only from one man.

When dabblers approach and are decoying well, a good rule is to let them come in as far as they will come until their feet are spread out and reaching for the water. Then, ducks farther away should be shot at first. If you do this, you'll have more birds in range longer.

Let's take two instances. First, the wrong way: Joe and Tom are decoying mallards. Here comes a flock of greenheads, and so they both work on them first with highballs, then feeding chuckles. The birds start in, with the leaders 25 yards out and the tail-enders out there at 35 to 40 yards but closing. The birds are intent on coming in, but both men jump and start shooting at the birds 25 yards away. They drop one each while those mallards 40 yards out flare and are out of range almost instantly.

Instance two: Joe and Tom work the flock with their calls and the birds come in the same way. But this time they stand and start shooting at the ducks 40 yards out, still in range and coming in. They drop one of these apiece. Meanwhile, the ducks that were 25 yards away have flared at the shots and movement and have started up, exposing their vitals. They are now at 35 yards and rising, but still in good range. The boys take two more. The total is four in this instance, simply because they took the longer shots first.

Furthermore, the birds out there at 40 yards will be less apt to see movement and flare, making them perhaps easier targets than those in close and able to see everything. In addition, ducks fairly well out—but still in good range—are less disturbed and present more head-on shots, where you have a chance of centering them in the head and neck and thus killing them cleanly. Long shots at going-away birds should be avoided. Such shots

Do you take them now? Do you wait for another pass? The age-old problem of water-fowling—are they coming in and if they aren't, are they in range? Photo by Steven Griffin.

may be easy to make, or hit, but the birds will most likely be crippled and go unrecovered.

Jump shooting requires a quick hand and a gun stocked to shoot a little high, say about a foot high at 40 yards. This is because dabblers you flush are likely to jump straight up, and so vertical lead is required. If your gun shoots "dead on," you'll need to completely cover a jumping duck to connect. A high-shooting gun allows you to swing up and fire as you come even with the bird. The lead is "built-in."

Whenever possible, and it almost always *is* possible, hold for the bird's head. Look for the face patch on a Canada, the green of a drake mallard's head or some other feature on the mark. Driving shot into the head and neck of a duck or goose will ensure a quick kill with only a few shot, whereas it may take multiple hits with big shot in the body to effect that result.

Waterfowl can really move. Unlike with upland birds, there is usually nothing nearby that you can use to gauge speed. And when decoying, the birds normally will have wings set or almost set and there isn't even the commotion of wingbeats to give you a hint at how fast the bird is moving.

Range judgment can also be difficult unless you pay attention to how the decoys have been set and have placed an "outer marker" block to signal when the ducks have moved within that magic 40-yard distance. All of these things conspire to make the waterfowler pull off the classic damnit-I-shot-behind miss.

The first double I ever pulled off, as a 17-year-old, happened under such circumstances. John Stevens and I were just picking up our blocks—early, because there was no action—when four mallards, three drakes and a Suzy, buzzed across left to right about 35 yards out and moving. I pulled up my 12-gauge auto, swung ahead of the lead duck, slapped the trigger, and the tail-end bird dropped. I swung ahead of the leader still farther, and the second duck in line, another drake, dropped. It seemed as if I was 15 feet in front on the second shot, but I would have been behind by three feet and missed but for a hapless greenhead who chose the wrong place in line. I congratulated myself out loud on shooting only drakes and sent the dog for the birds. Stevens didn't believe I planned it then, and I'm sure he knows about my dumb luck now.

Geese present real problems for the novice. First, they are so big that they look in range when they are still 100 yards out. Secondly, a Canada can really move—deceptively so. I've watched geese, seemingly lumbering along, pass mallards that were flapping like the devil was astride them. I've missed geese that passed low over the water by shooting 10 feet behind. As a matter of fact, I've missed about everything on this continent by shooting behind at one time or another.

Estimating range is best done by the Old Hickory Jackson method: When you can see their eyes, they're in range. Usually, when I *hope* they're in range, they're not. Some things you just know, and when I *know* birds are in range, they are. Hoping gets me into trouble most days.

The rule for getting enough forward allowance on birds is to swing like hell. The best method, for me, anyway, is to start behind the bird, swing along its line of flight faster than the bird is traveling, and fire when the muzzle passes the bird; not *as* it passes, but *after* it passes. I'll do the same thing on long-range crossing shots, only I won't fire until I've passed the duck by what looks to be the length of the bird's body. This method seems to work well and it works faster than the "pointing out" method, where you establish lead and move the muzzle at the same speed ahead of the bird and then fire. If you are moving the muzzle of the gun when you pass the bird, your chances of a hit are increased. If you stop the muzzle, you'll miss—period.

Sometimes, however, a smooth swing isn't going to get the job done. In flooded timber, for instance, shooting at spots is about the best you'll get as far as an opportunity goes. In these cases you're best off to take a leaf from the notebook of the brush shooter and pick a bird, swing through quickly, and touch off without stopping. Normally, birds coming into flooded timber offer tricky shots, so the ticket is to shoot quickly without stopping your swing.

Speaking of picking a bird, the beginner often falls prey to the flock-shooting malady. A large contingent of ducks drops in, and you stand and fire. Later, while fishing your empties out of the water as your partner's dog is retrieving *his* birds, it dawns on you that you didn't pick out a specific bird and go after him. Oh sure, you looked at all of 'em—twice. You just didn't shoot at one. This can be especially frustrating when it's a flock of geese and they seem to be hanging there above your blocks like so many kites. You stand, blaze away, and then they all fly away. Terrible.

The wind can affect your shooting, and it can work to your advantage. As noted earlier, when panicked, waterfowl will most likely take the quickest way out, and this means they'll use the wind. As they land into the wind, let them come in as far as possible before you stand to shoot. This way, when they flare back with the wind, they will be flaring back across your field of fire, giving you additional opportunities. Remember to lead birds that are flying into the wind almost as much as those flying with it because the shot string will be pushed back. And lead even more on cold days, because the shotshell won't be as efficient—the load won't move as fast—as it will on warm days.

For chokes on the waterfowl gun, we first have to consider loads. The science of shotshell manufacture is almost at the point where chokes can be labeled a moot point. Hard lead shot, perhaps copper-plated to resist barrel deformation and buffered with a granulated plastic to combat the squeezing deformation that takes place at ignition, patterns tightly in any barrel.

When the trigger is pulled, the instant acceleration of the shot charge causes some shot (they aren't called "pellets") in the middle of the shot column to be deformed—flattened. These do not travel true and tend to fly away from and lag behind the rest of the shot charge as it travels through the air. Other shot are scrubbed flat by the barrel, especially as they pass through the constriction of the choke in the end of the barrel. These also become "flyers," and are of little use in killing a duck.

Using hard shot combats these forces, and adding a buffering agent helps eliminate some of the "setback deformation" as well. Hard shot and buffering agents in a maximum-load 12-gauge shell make these the most efficient loads ever developed for shooting waterfowl.

Alas, about the time that these became known on the market, the whole spectre of lead-shot poisoning of waterfowl reared its ugly head. In the Federal Refuges and in most state refuges, steel shot—"non-toxic"—is the law, and with that law came a whole new set of problems for both hunters and shell manufacturers.

Waterfowl have a nasty habit of picking up spent shot from the bottoms of ponds, lakes and rivers, thinking it's grit. The lead has a nasty habit of killing them when they do that. So, it has become increasingly evident that shooting non-toxic shot—and steel is the best choice—is the only way to go.

The steel vs. lead shot argument is still raging today, although it has died down a bit. The crux of the argument was that steel, being lighter and less efficient than lead, tended to cripple birds. Is it better to cripple with steel or to poison with lead?

Well, crippling is a self-inflicted wound on waterfowlers. Crippling, to a great extent, can be avoided through the proper understanding and use of steel loads. Lead poisoning is something that will happen, regardless, in areas where lead is used and birds ingest it.

So the argument is rendered invalid. We can eliminate a lot of the steel shot crippling at the same time we can eliminate lead poisoning. The problem with poisoning is that birds thus afflicted become mink bait and aren't observed by waterfowlers; the cripples are observed.

Since steel shot is the law of the land in many areas, let's take a look at the dynamics of this load and the chokes and sizes that will prove most effective on waterfowl.

Steel, being harder, isn't subject to quite the same laws of physics as lead. It doesn't deform and it travels faster, but it's also lighter and thus each shot hits with less energy, shot-for-shot, than lead, and so it penetrates and kills less efficiently.

Another reason for shooters downgrading steel shot is that you have to shoot steel differently than you do lead.

Essentially, steel shot starts off faster than lead because it *is* lighter. But, once it's out 25 yards or so, the speed falls off more rapidly than lead, and thus at long range—40 to 45 yards—it is moving slower than lead would be.

Most shooters, having a hunting career in which their minds have factored in the way to lead with and hit with lead, miss consistently with this load until they've made the mental adjustments. Basically, the adjustments call for you to allow less lead with steel on close-in targets, and give more forward allowance with steel than you would with lead once you're out past 25 to 30 yards.

The shotgun is a short-range shooter, and steel makes the range even shorter. It will cripple at extreme ranges, but then so will lead shot. The ticket to effective use of steel shot is to become a better caller, a better blind-builder and a better setter of decoys so that birds will come in closer and allow you to take advantage of the shorter forward allowances offered by steel shot.

In truth most duck hunters, when compared with expert grouse hunters and quail shooters, are not all that great with a smoothbore. Some are downright pathetic. I think that part of the reason for this is that the conditions under which we water-fowlers shoot are usually abominable: tossing seas, unstable footing, guns heavier than we'd like, a Lab that smacks you upside the head about the time you draw down, wind, rain, snow, sleet, long ranges, a mark that's moving with speed incoming, outgoing, pant . . . pant. . . .

All of these things conspire to rob a good field shot of his chance to become a legend amongst his peers. Couple this with the fact that a shooter may sit all day in the driving rain while his muscles stiffen up, and then have his entire day's net worth of action take place in the last 45 seconds of fading sunlight, and you can see why it takes years of practice to turn in even re-spectable scores on waterfowl.

In choosing a choke for waterfowling, I think first you have to look at whether you'll be shooting steel or lead shot. You may end up shooting both over the course of a season, depending upon the restrictions where you hunt. If you are going to be shooting lead, I think that a good, tight-patterning load of buff-ered shot fired through a tight improved cylinder barrel is just the ticket for hunting over decoys. The short-magnum shell in 12-gauge that holds one- and a-half ounces of shot—and here I'd choose No. 6 lead—through an improved cylinder barrel gives you a wide, dense pattern that's effective out to 40 yards. If you aren't that sure of yourself or you think that the ranges will be a tad longer, go for the standard one- and one-quarter-ounce load and a modified barrel with lead shot.

For geese, using lead shot, I have to say that the best bet in my experiences is a good load of No. 2 shot and a full choke. This combination usually patterns pretty well in most barrels, and goose shooting can get to be a 45- to 50-yard affair pretty regularly. You're going to want something that will reach out and touch them, as the phone company used to say.

If you're hunting in flooded timber most of the time and you don't go after your birds until they're at treetop height, pick the improved cylinder barrel and a fast load of No. 6 backed up with a similar load in No. 4. After the first shot, the birds will be packing it out of there, and the extra range of a No. 4 can be helpful—although with a tight improved cylinder barrel, things get skimpy out past 40 yards.

Pass shooting with lead shot calls for either a tight modified or full choke because of the ranges involved, and for ducks I'd stick with No. 4s.

With steel shot, the research is pretty conclusive that steel behaves less efficiently than lead. After that, things get fuzzy.

Steel loads come in shot sizes which approximate, as much as possible, lead loads one step down. In other words, steel 4s behave a lot like lead 6s. The new steel shot loads are nothing at all like the original ones, which were like shooting, as someone said, "daisy petals." Still, the facts of physics can't be denied, and the fact is that after 45 yards, any steel-load kill reflects the fate of a patently unlucky duck.

Given that steel's velocity falls off at or before 45 yards, then, it is silly for anyone to shoot steel shot through a full-choked barrel, and the reason is clear: Full choke is at its best after 40 yards. Under that distance, modified is better because it provides a more even pattern distribution. After that distance, at the point when full choke should really come into its own—and does, with lead shot—there isn't enough energy left in the light steel shot to make it a killer anyway. It's somewhat similar to having a 10-power scope on a .22 rimfire rifle—where the scope would be useful, the load is ineffective.

The harder steel patterns well with modified barrels, as a general rule. With improved cylinder barrels, the patterns get too sketchy at 40 yards with steel to make this a worthwhile boring. But modified seems to be like Baby Bear's porridge: it's about right for all conditions under which you're likely to shoot a duck.

Steel, being lighter, is more affected by crosswinds, don't

forget, and this has to be worked into the mental computer when establishing forward allowance, but don't forget that steel needs *less* forward allowance than lead close in, and *more* farther out.

Other things specifically having to do with shotguns should probably be talked about here, so I will. I like those old, WWII steel ammunition boxes for holding shells. They're real rupture-makers when they're full, but they can take the abuse, although they sound like the hammers of hell when you knock one over in a canoe just as the blacks are decoying.

I also like a sling on a waterfowl gun, even if the sling is fastened in some manner to the gun case. I usually have my hands full of stuff all the time when I'm loading/unloading, so a sling makes good sense.

If you do much hunting by tidal flats, remember to give your gun a good bath in a good-quality oil after each hunt. Even a bright day along the ocean will have salt-laden spray to some degree, so take care of your gun accordingly.

Of the variable choking devices on the market, the screw-in models are the best. Many of the earlier variable choke models featured the sleeved tube that could be cranked down or up but many times didn't shoot the way they were supposed to. The screw-in chokes, offered as standard equipment on some guns, can give you a pocketful of shotgun barrels with very little effort. If your pet gun isn't so equipped, you might want to check with a gunsmith who specializes in installing screw-in chokes. The best part about these is that they really—pretty much—shoot the patterns you want. The modified tube shoots modified, and the full, in the better models, shoots full. They're slick.

Any good duck gun should be fitted with a recoil pad. Even a slip-on pad is better than none, and these can be taken off so the gun still fits if weather necessitates thicker clothing. Recoil reducers in the stock are a godsend for those who are kick-conscious.

Another contraption that helps reduce recoil is called the Recoil Shock Eliminator, manufactured by The Sportsman Company in Davison, Michigan. This is a pad that goes inside your shooting coat and hangs down against the area where your stock comes, held in place by a Velcro closure that's sewed into the garment. Sam Johnson, the manufacturer, tells me that recoil-conscious shooters have considered this a real shoulder-saver, especially waterfowlers who use magnum loads. Trapshooters love it too.

Sam sent me a set of these—three different thicknesses—and I tried them all. I even had my two boys try them. Chris is a rugged 12-year-old with a lot of shooting experience, and he loved his; Jason is 9 and new to shooting, but he said that his 20-gauge felt more like a .410 when he used the magnum pad at the skeet range. Since these kids can both outshoot me already, I kept the pads for myself. Why give them another advantage—youth and coordination ought to be enough.

In the matter of gun fit, waterfowlers could stand to take a lesson or two from their upland counterparts. The fit on a waterfowl gun would be about right—and there would be more good shooters—if the stocks were a little longer and straighter (less drop at comb and heel) than they are. As a rule, you've got a little more time to get your cheek down on a duck gun than you do on a grouse gun because the need for *real* speed isn't that critical. Resultantly, you can get your cheek down and make good use of a straight stock's virtues: less felt recoil, and a gun that will shoot a little higher, enabling you to swing better and get a view of what's going on without lifting your face to get a look. And, since most waterfowling is done by shooting at a mark that's above you, a high-shooting stock makes sense because it allows you to get some built-in vertical lead.

If your stock is a little too high, you won't shoot it well, and some judicious use of sandpaper and perhaps a wood rasp followed by a refinishing job can bring things right into line.

Although I like a straight grip on an upland gun, I'll take a pistol grip on a waterfowling piece simply because it seems to "steer" better with cold hands. I once had an autoloader that I had straight-gripped and the results were disastrous to my shooting—even worse than normal.

A rib on a pump or auto is almost a necessity as well. It keeps accumulations of snow and water off the sighting plane better than a plain barrel, and it makes a nice, broad highway out there for shooting, even though you and I will *swear* we don't see the barrel when we're shooting. We wouldn't lie, would we?

While we're talking about shooting, I just want to stress—

as I've done before—the importance of practice. Aside from trap and skeet shooting, which always help you hone the old shooting eye, I'd say that spending a day at a hunting preserve that features flighted-mallard shooting is a real education.

First let me clear up a few things about shooting preserves— game farms, to some. These operations offer shoot-for-pay hunting, normally for upland birds such as pheasants, quail and chukars. But some also offer waterfowl hunting, and flighted mallards are the targets when that's the case.

Shooting preserves can be as tame or as wild as the hunter wants, and they vary from open-to-the-public outfits to swank members-only operations. The quality of the hunting doesn't depend on the price of the hunt, but on the operator's personal viewpoint of things.

Preserves are a great way to do several things. As dog-training facilities, they're tops. Likewise for training youngsters. And, since most states allow preserves to open a little earlier and stay open a little longer than the regular hunting seasons, they are a fine way to get more shooting each year.

On the minus side, they cost money, but then don't tell me you do your waterfowling for free once you factor in licenses, stamps, shells, gas, boats, dogs, dog food, decoys, clothing. . . .

While I've found that the upland hunting on a preserve can sometimes leave a bit to be desired, the waterfowl hunting is almost universally pretty good. Flighted-mallard shooting is, in fact, one of the toughest forms of shooting presently found on this or any nearby planet. Here's how it works.

Ducks are trained to fly to a pond where they are fed. They're kept in a cage or enclosure on one end of the preserve's grounds, usually, and the pond where they feed is on the other end. Each day, normally twice a day, they are released from the enclosure by way of a ramp that leads to a tower. The little beggars simply trundle up the ramp to the top of the tower, jump into space and fly to the pond; it's all in the training, you know.

Somewhere between the tower and the pond are positioned some blinds. This is where the plot thickens. The ducks leave the tower heading for the pond. Once they pick up steam, they are about in the area where the blinds are located. By this time, because they started out high, they are up maybe 35 to 40 yards.

Since they are well-conditioned for flight, they're also moving like hell. They're tough, believe me. The shooting is, of course, pass shooting, and the cost of a duck may be from $10 up. But since the unshot birds can be used over and over—they don't leave the grounds—it isn't like upland hunting on a preserve, where you pay for all birds released.

This is a great place to train a youngster and give him or her that first, important exposure to shooting. The conditions can be tightly controlled by you and the manager of the club, and ducks can be released in flocks or singles. You have time to teach, look for mistakes and hone skills.

The same can be said for dog training. Again, the controlled conditions make for easier training under "real" circumstances, and a preserve not only lets you start a young dog earlier, it also adds many days afield for an old campaigner who just may not be able to stand the rigors of a cold day in an offshore blind as he once did.

In the chapter called "The Future of the Sport," some of the reasons why waterfowlers drop out of the sport are examined. But right now, I'd like to talk a little about getting kids started early in duck hunting. The statistics show that the earlier a boy/ girl gets introduced to waterfowling, the more likely he/she is to stick with it.

I've got three children, with the younger two being boys who love hunting and the outdoors. My daughter, frankly, is convinced that there's something a little unmasculine about boys her age who hate hunting. (Heh, heh, heh.) Anyway, the education of a waterfowl hunter should start early with duck identification, helping the Old Man work the dog, repainting decoys and trips to the marsh during the off-season—like the spring migration—to look at ducks and geese. These things build the appreciation.

When they are the right age, and that's up to you, the kids should be introduced to firearms, safety first, then eventually to shooting. I started my boys by shooting wind-blown balloons on a pond with a 22 loaded with birdshot. This mini-shotshell is easy to hit with, has no recoil and makes a big deal about breaking the balloon.

Next comes the shotgun, and a 20-gauge is the way to go.

Forget the 410—it's too hard to hit with for a kid. Get a 20 and add a recoil pad or a recoil reducer of some sort. Take the youngster to the gun club's skeet field and stand at station 7; from here, have straightaways (low houses) thrown until a few are powdered, then quit. Expand the time spent shooting each trip, then have some station 7 high houses added. These require a little lead and teach swing and follow-through. Then, when you and the youngster feel pretty good about things, take a full round of skeet.

The next step should be to a shooting preserve, if you have one handy. If yours has no mallard shooting, take some upland birds. Let the young hunter shoot a bird *before* the first day in the blind with a gun.

Now, I assume you've allowed the youngster to come along without a gun when you've been duck hunting. This builds interest and also shows him what it's like out there. But once he is hunting, do your best to keep your eye on him and allow him that first shot whenever possible. After the first season, let him know that it's up to him to be ready and take his own birds—he's now a full partner, and probably the best you'll ever have.

8

The Gear

If there's a more gadget-oriented segment of the sporting populace than waterfowlers, I sure haven't met any of them unless you want to count trout fishermen—and I don't.

It seems as if no duck hunter is satisfied unless he has at least two of everything and a backup in case something goes wrong with the pair he has, one of which he never uses anyhow.

So it goes with ducking. I think part of the reason, aside from the normal fascination with "stuff," concerns the conditions under which we hunt. These conditions can be so life-threatening, on occasion, that without the proper gear there might not be a tomorrow.

In the matter of boats, some hunters opt for a deep-V style

measuring 14 to 16 feet long. Others like the old Boston whaler style, while others prefer a sneakboat with enclosed gunwales. But day in and day out, I think it's tough to beat the flexibility of a good aluminum canoe painted dead-grass color with a square stern for an outboard motor—and make mine about 17 feet.

Such a craft handles easily, can be staked out for use as a blind (see Chapter 3 for rigging a stake-out setup), goes places where a V-bottom won't, and with some muscles, even one man can hoist it on and off a cartop carrier. Such a rig works even best if it's on a trailer, however. Then you can fill it with decoys and other gear, lash a tarp over the whole mess, and be gone. If you are primarily a diver hunter, go for a 16-foot V.

A canoe can be concealed with little difficulty, and you can paddle the thing quite easily if your kicker won't kick over. And here, I'd recommend a 5- to 7-h.p. outboard of a good brand for taking care of this chore. Such an engine really moves a craft along, with more than enough speed for most circumstances.

I wouldn't suggest a canoe for much deepwater work, but aside from that, this craft will take most of the work you'll be dishing out. Whenever we talk about water craft, we have to discuss safety too. Let me tell you a little story that involves me and a fellow I've mentioned before, John Stevens. Twenty years later, I can still make him shiver by saying, "Remember the day we went over?" If you look up the word "stupid" in the dictionary, there's a picture of Stevens and me.

It was the last day of the duck season, and a late-November gale was blowing as we put off in John's canoe for an afternoon shoot. The spray turned to ice on our clothing before we even had the blocks set out, but we were young, enthusiastic and probably not overly-bright. We had some good shooting, but the cold and horizontal snow finally got to us, so we picked up early, with maybe an hour of daylight left.

We were in about seven feet of water and were paddling the canoe out of the blind (where it had been only about two feet deep). We had just started toward the spread of decoys when a mallard came across the water low—very low, fighting the gale. As he got closer, he veered more and more to the right. Badly wanting that fat greenhead, I swiveled in the front seat to swing

The canoe is a top craft for most duck shooting. It can be the basis for a blind or the means of transportation for a float trip, and it's light and maneuverable. Photo by Steven Griffin.

with him, but he was moving too fast and I couldn't catch up. Being right-handed, I was in the process of binding myself up by swinging too far to the right.

I was shooting one of those little glass-barreled 12-gauge Model 59 Winchesters, and it only weighed about six- and one-half pounds. Being a young stallion with big forearms from my college boxing days, I continued the swing with my right hand, pistol style, and touched her off.

That spiteful little autoloader came crashing back against my chest, and I was dimly aware that the mallard was skipping across the water, stone dead. I didn't have long to congratulate myself, though, because several things happened at once, all of them bad.

In fact, it was almost as if it happened in slow motion. The recoil jarred me backward, so Stevens, in the stern, used his weight to correct. Now John was a football tackle in those days, and he not only had the strength, but the weight as well. When he corrected for the recoil in an attempt to balance the craft, he *corrected*.

When he corrected, I corrected the opposite way for *his* correction, and the whole damned canoe started to slosh from side to side. As if the human frailties weren't enough, the wind started to work on the botton of the canoe each time she came out of the water. Finally, after what seemed like minutes of this seagoing seesaw, the logical conclusion to youthful lack of vision reared up and bit us: We both corrected on the same side of the canoe at the same time—I still say Stevens did it—and over we went.

We had no lifejackets, no flotation cushions and—evidently—no brains. We went straight to the bottom. Didn't pass GO or collect $200 or anything; we just ditched. I still held my auto, and Johnny had grabbed his Browning on the way down, but that's all we saved. We lost a lantern, about six boxes of shells (when you're young, you're not only a lousy shot, you're also an optimist), two thermos bottles, duck calls and everything else that wasn't tied down—and nothing was.

In seven feet of water, you take a long time to come up. For all the clothing we had on, we were lucky. John and I were both strong swimmers and were unafraid of the water. You fight your natural instincts and let training take over: "Don't panic, relax, you'll float to the surface." Only you don't. Both of us had to fight our way up and latch onto the canoe, now belly up and bobbing in the whitecaps.

Somehow, we both still had our guns, which we quickly unloaded, the shells clanging their way across the aluminum hull and to a place with their brethren in the deep. Stevens looked at me and said something succinct, like, "Smitty, you sonuvabitch." Then I started to laugh. John started to laugh too, and the whole canoe started rocking again. There we were, a mile from help in the middle of a November gale, clinging to an overturned canoe in seven feet of water, sopping wet, slowly freezing to death, laughing like idiots.

Well, we righted the canoe, and I sloshed in and used my hat to bail out enough water so that John could get in too. We found one paddle, and John took us to shore. It was a long way in, and many times, when I've been cold while duck hunting, I've remembered that ride and told myself, "No, Dummy, you've been colder." We got back to the launch area, and ice fell off us in sheets. It's a wonder we didn't get frostbite or hypothermia.

Since that time, I don't go in a boat—winter or summer—that doesn't have a flotation device for every occupant. One of those camo-colored flotation vests is great, especially for the ride to and from the hunting area. If it hampers your shooting, take it off and sit on it, but keep it handy. Make sure someone always knows where you're going to be hunting and what time you expect to be home. I always give a "Worry time." I say something like: "I'm going duck hunting. I should be back an hour after dark, which will be about 7:30 p.m. If I'm not back by 9:00 p.m., I'm probably in trouble." It's handy.

One of those little flare guns that only weighs a few ounces is great to have with you, too. I'd suggest you stow it in a watertight container and carry it on you, not in the canoe.

If you are going for some wilderness backwater jump shooting, leave a note on the windshield of your car with your expected time back on it. That way, the cops'll have a place to start looking.

I also always carry a compass with me, especially if I'm hunting a new area of big water. Things have a way of getting turned around, and after you've picked up the blocks and darkness is closing in on you, you may lose your bearings. A compass works if you look at it going *in* so you'll know which way is *out*. I get lost easily, much to the consternation of my pals, so a compass goes with me everywhere. If I didn't feel ridiculous, I'd take one with me to the john.

Decoys have been discussed before, but I'll just say a few more words about them. They are an important part of the whole operation, and you should "cull your flock" carefully. Any that are worn should be painted and reconditioned. Those that don't float well or list to one side should be tossed out, and keels and lines should be checked carefully.

One way of fastening the lines to the body when picking up is to use a large loop of rubber attached to the weight. Wrap the line around the keel and then stretch the rubber across the keel to secure the whole shebang. It works, even when you're wearing gloves.

Painting decoys is a middle-of-the-summer operation, and one that isn't that bad of a chore; in fact, it's rather enjoyable—and it sure beats cutting the grass in your waders to stay in touch with your feelings about waterfowling. Take your time and only hit the high spots with the brush. Attempts at real art are wasted on the ducks, the setup of the blocks being more important than their color.

Staying alive in a duck blind and still staying concealed is a function of clothing. I wear waders almost all the time, the only exception being when I'm doing some jump shooting in backwaters—and then it's hipboots. I wear insulated waders even during the early season, rather than uninsulated ones, because while I may be 5 feet 10 inches tall, I only weigh about 150 pounds, and am always about half-frozen anyway.

Make sure that the soles of your waders or hippers don't get worn and smooth with age, because then you're asking for a dunking. I like to alternate between two pairs of waders. I find that two alternated pairs last longer, in total, than two pairs worn until first one pair is worn out, and then the other. In this case, the whole is greater than the sum of its parts. I know, it doesn't add up.

Also, when I'm hunting a lot, I find that a pair of waders needs a full 24 hours to thoroughly dry out. This way I always have a dry pair waiting in the wings. One of these days I'll get a pair of those electric boot dryers.

Under the waders, I wear a pair of corduroy pants with rubber bands around the cuffs to keep them from riding up. Corduroy is warm, soft, supple, and it breathes. Nothing else seems to work quite so well for me; maybe they'll do well for you, too.

Since ducks are *not* color blind, you have to avoid any loud shades in what you wear. I like a good, waterproof insulated parka over a turtleneck shirt and wool sweater. If it's really cold, I start off with long underwear, insulated, with dress socks. Then comes a pair of wool socks—just one. Too many socks will bind your feet and they'll go numb on you. Then come the cords, T-neck, sweater, parka and waders.

A Jones-style ducking hat with earflaps, in camouflage, tops off the outfit. If I expect foul weather—and I always expect foul weather—I'll take along a full-length camouflaged rain slicker. This can also work as a windbreaker if the breeze is especially bitey.

For gloves, I use two pairs. Light cotton gloves covered with a large pair of rubber ones with big, watercatching gauntlets are great for setting out and picking up decoys. Once in the blind, I switch to a pair of wool gloves with no leather on them. Wool, as you know, is about the only natural fiber that stays warm even when wet; it does that for sheep, by the way, which is probably why they grow it. So, even though these gloves will no doubt get soggy by day's end, they're still warm. Carry an extra pair if you think of it.

Some men I've hunted with wear face nets or paint their faces so as to avoid that shine that screams *human* to overhead birds. I just keep my head down. I can't stand the stuff, so I just try to be more careful. If you can bear to wear these things, do it. I'm sure they work.

Among the other pieces of equipment that duckers should consider are little heaters that you can take inside a blind with you. Even a charcoal broiler or grill is good because it can be used to heat up a sandwich. One of the slickest things I've seen involves a large can, like a No. 10 oil can, a roll of toilet paper and alcohol. Soak the paper in alcohol, drop it in the can, and set a match to it. The thing burns for hours and gives off a cheery bit of heat to warm your numb little body. Just be careful when you jump up to shoot. Catalytic heaters, available from outlets specializing in camping equipment, are probably the best.

For duck camps, or for the man who hunts with a large party most of the time, an automated duck plucker is a godsend. These contraptions quickly and efficiently take off the feathers that would take you and me hours. The vacuum attachments keep the feathers in a bag instead of in the neighbor's shrubbery. They are expensive, but worth it if you're going to be cleaning a lot of birds (and we all hope we will be).

I use maps to indicate the areas I like to hunt, especially the backcountry sloughs and slow streams that I like to float. Having your maps laminated at an office-supply outlet saves wear and tear, and storing them, rolled up, in a cardboard tube is a good form of safekeeping. These tubes can usually be begged off merchants who sell you prints. Pay for a tube only under protest.

One of the toughest things the human body is asked to do is to unload a stack of decoys, untrailer a boat, and take care of all the other odds and ends associated with waterfowling while it's still dark out. This is further complicated by the fact that about the only way to see what's going on is by holding a flashlight in your mouth. This can be a difficult feat, so not long ago, I hit on the idea of using the little nightlights that flyfishermen use for tying on their hunks of feathers in pitch darkness.

These lights fasten to a shirt pocket with a spring clip, and with their flexible goose-neck heads, they can be pointed wherever you want the light. They aren't cheap, but a good one will take years of abuse. The batteries last a long time, and they are about the handiest thing I've found for the early/late evening hours.

Another good light to have along is the fluorescent lantern type. I've got one with a single fluorescent bulb, a spot beam and a yellow emergency flasher. It's rugged and serves double duty as a good travel light in my hunting car. You can turn one of these babies on and work for hours without exhausting the batteries.

Speaking of cars, most family members won't climb into the duckhunter's car unless there's an offer of financial reward for the act—especially during the season. If you can swing it, a separate car for yourself and the dog makes good sense. I have a station wagon with a standard four-speed transmission, and it locks into four-wheel-drive with the flip of a lever. It has high clearance, during the gunning season I can put down the back seat and easily load the tons of assorted gear that accompany autumn sports.

Where I hunt, the opportunity presents itself to do some early-morning duck hunting followed by some midday grouse hunting, followed by a trip back to the marsh for the afternoon flights. So, the gunning car has to hold an assortment of stuff—plus a patient little setter who waits for us to quit fooling around on the water and get serious. I also stash a sleeping bag in the car, because I've been known to stay a little later than planned a time or two, and the bag has been a lifesaver.

A pickup with a cap is a good alternative to my wagon, and so is a standard 4×4 such as those offered by all the major manufacturers. Even a standard full-sized wagon has good weight distribution and traction. But if you're serious about water-fowling, eventually you'll end up with a 4×4. They're tough to beat.

The gunning car also holds dry clothes, including socks and moccasins. I've found that riding home with dry footgear and a down jacket makes the whole sport a little more civilized. You can stand the rest of you being wet for a while, so long as your extremities are warm, and the feet have to be the first thing considered.

A set of hand tools is always good to have along. With all the things that can go wrong with guns, boat trailers and dog kennels, I'm surprised more shooters don't pack tools. I'll bet, on an average morning at the local refuge parking lot, I could rent out a pair of pliers enough times to put one of my kids through Dartmouth. Somebody always needs something.

Another handy gadget to have is a pair of binoculars. I started carrying some with me a couple of years ago, and they have remarkable uses. You can see how many decoys the other guy has out, sneer at his spread and lack of imagination, and laugh at his choice of shotguns. You can also watch him pick up early with his limit.

There are lulls during any hunt, and binoculars come in handy then to scan the sky for ducks and other forms of wildlife. I'm a real bird fancier—keep a feeding station all winter and the whole nine yards, so I love watching the bird life that abounds in the marsh. An Audubon bird guide or one by Roger Tory Peterson helps, too. These are made to slide into a hip pocket, and I pull mine out when a new species flits by. Nobody accuses me of being effete about it, either, but then I'm always armed.

Binoculars come under the category of things that help pass the time and aren't really necessary, but we could possibly say the same thing about waterfowling in general, couldn't we?

My pal Charlie has a trailer that holds everything he needs for ducking. He carries his decoys, stake-out materials described earlier, assorted whatnot, and he throws his two canoes on top of the whole thing. As I mentioned before, having two canoes—with one being the dory that carries the gear—is a good idea. This trailer has wide swinging doors and interior lights for helping in the early morning and at night. The guns and dogs go into Charlie's station wagon, of course, but the trailer keeps the wet and muddy items separate from the humans as much as possible. It's a good idea, and if the expense of such a rig is too much for you, simply split the cost with a partner.

Finally, any good gun takes one hell of a beating in a duck boat. I swear by my smooth old Model 12 Winchester, the finest waterfowling gun ever built, in my opinion. But by the end of a season, it looks as if somebody used it for a crowbar. So, every once in a while, a stock refinishing job is in order. Now a gunsmith will charge you a pretty sum for this service, and that's fine. On the other hand, you can also do a passable job yourself and have a good, non-glare finish besides.

Start by stripping off the old finish, what's left of it, by using a strong commercial stripping agent that's advertised to take off paint and varnish. Next, sand the stock smooth with medium, then very fine, sandpaper. If you have any dents in the stock—and you will—wet these and then raise the wood by judicious application of a steam iron. Sand out the edges of the dent.

After sanding, wet the stock and heat it over a low gas flame. This brings up the "whiskers" of the wood, so you can sand them off with fine sandpaper.

Now, buy some spar varnish and apply a light coat to the stock. Let this coat dry at least a full day, preferably two. Then, using the fine sandpaper again, sand off the spar varnish as completely as you can without violating the wood grain. What you've done is seal the pores of the wood. You can repeat this step if you want, but it's probably not necessary.

Next, get a bottle of linseed oil or a mixture called by the tradename "Linspeed." Put some on your fingertips and rub it into the stock in a circular motion. Rub the stock until it's warm, a little at a time, and then palm rub the whole stock. Let this coat dry completely for at least 24 hours, then use some very fine steel wool to work it down. Repeat with another application, and then another. You can keep this up until the next Ice Age, but after about a half-dozen coats, the stock is about as protected as it's going to get, so you might as well quit.

What you now have is an oil-finished stock, the very best finish there is. An oil finish doesn't glare like a neon sign, it looks rich, and if you scratch it, just take some oil and rub it into the wound. Good as new. The checkering can be cleaned with an old toothbrush—or that of your mother-in-law, if the old girl lives with you—dipped in the stripping agent, but every three or four years you may want a gunsmith to cut you a new patch of diamonds. Checkering has a way of smoothing out with the years, and after a time it becomes useless. I'd suggest nothing finer than 20 lines to the inch. This still looks nice, yet gives a good gripping surface.

David Gareth Roebuck

9

Etcetera

As far as I know, you may be reading this in the year 2066 in the attic of your Uncle Dexter because the old gent just up and died, and at one time he hunted ducks so you decided to sneak up and see what you could boost before the will was read and your cousin Julius made macramé out of his gunning coat.

If that's the case, the very fact that this volume survived that long should make it near and dear to your heart. Because if it has, then you are in possession of part of the memorabilia of waterfowling.

I walked into the house the other day, muddy from a day of researching this book and getting sat on by a wet Lab, and there, standing before me, was my 16-year-old daughter, Amy. She was off to a school dance, and she was wearing a sweater

100

with a mallard on it, a turtleneck under that, resplendent with beige canvasbacks rampant on a background of burgundy, and a belt that sported an Abercrombie & Fitch brass duck head. Upon her elfin feet were what you and I used to call "field shoes," and what she and her cohorts call "duck shoes"—little loafer-style, rubber-bottomed, leather-topped moccasins.

I stood there and swiftly calculated how much it cost me to dress this child in that manner, and then reflected upon how kids used to throw a blanket over us when their friends came over and we still had on our ducking clothes. No more, at least right at this place and space in time. Ducks—and duck hunting, by implication—are now chic.

For a long time, ducks were the quarry of the rich. Today, maidens from the concrete canyons of New York are bedecked in the styles of L.L. Bean, et al., and those styles dictate the wearing of the greenhead. This selfsame daughter, who labels me an "over-aged Preppie," is now smitten herself. Her closet looks like a federal refuge after a three-day blow.

Wherever I go, I'm inundated by ducks on paperweights, ladies' blouses, men's lapels, water faucets, whiskey glasses (no complaints here) and anything else the makers figure the marks out there will buy.

But this fad will pass, I'm sure. The guilty will move onto something else, leaving us here to again count up our ducking collectibles and chortle like the king in his counting house. And when you think of it, the slice of Americana that is waterfowling is best reflected upon in the collectibles. Sometimes when I look at these pieces of history, I wonder if maybe I'm watching a present I love become part of the past. Then I go talk to my pal Jack Daniels and the feeling goes right away.

Among the notable collectibles are the decoys of the past, those carved by the workmanlike hands of such men as the Masons of Detroit fame, and other carvers who had the skill to impart a soft glow of life to a chunk of northern-white cedar. I still hope to find an old Mason in a garage sale someplace, but so far no luck. And with style being what it is, the chances of that happening diminish with each passing year.

Decoys used to be tools; today, they're an art form. The decorator decoys are a fine example. Craftsmen-artists spend hours on a single feather, months on a single decoy, and viewing

Decoy carving, once a functional craft, has evolved into an art form, with the top carvers commanding high prices for highly-detailed works. The best carvers are booked up years in advance. Photo by Steven Griffin.

these works will take your breath away, so real are they in proportion, coloring and pose. Competitions separate the carvers from the whittlers, and the best at this are booked up for years. My boys, Chris and Jake, are into decoy carving, and regularly open the odd artery or two.

Maybe a decade ago, I had a pal who had a fine string of cedar bluebill decoys. They were coated with many seasons of touch-up painting, but they were seaworthy and floated like the real things. I happened to mention that I thought they would be worth some money to a collector. Unfortunately for him, I mentioned this in front of his wife. Within two weeks, his decoys were no longer holding down the shelves in the shed next to his duck cabin on Lake Huron. Instead, they'd been parlayed into a new couch and 12 yards of carpeting. I remember him calling from duck camp to tell me of his misery over this turn of events. He ended by saying, through gritted teeth, "When I hang up the phone, I'm going to go outside and burn your sneakboat to the waterline." He did, too. I suppose I deserved it.

I was talking with a fellow the other day who allowed as how his wife and kids had given him one of those phones that looks like a decoy and quacks instead of rings. I think I like that.

Decoys, especially those which came from the hands and knives of some long-dead artisan, have always held a certain mellow charm unconcealed by paint or the passage of time. Each season, some poor ducker's string of decoys is ravaged by those who would peel off the keel and make a mantle ornament out of a working chunk of wood. But here the block gets the honor it deserves, rather than the marginal treatment which gave it that used look in the first place.

If decoys are the relics of the past and art of the present, what of the limited-edition print? Here, an entire industry has sprung up in which art reflects life. The likes of David Maass, Jim Foote, Maynard Reese and a host of others have brought the world of the waterfowler into the dens, offices and homes of waterfowlers throughout the world.

The joy of owning a limited-edition print comes from the fact that there are only a certain number of these in existence. They are signed by the artist, and given a number that tells which one it is, such as 244/850. Some people try to collect all the works of a particular artist in a certain number.

Such organizations as Ducks Unlimited (DU) and various state groups with similar, lofty aims of providing habitat for waterfowl thrive on the sale, at auction, of prints.

I like DU. I like the people involved with it, I like their aims, I like the way that they speak of waterfowl in almost reverent tones (most days, anyway).

I like DU banquets. I like wandering around and looking at the tables of prizes and auction items, knowing that I'll probably win a box of dog chewies or something equally exotic, but dreaming of winning big anyway. I like listening to the talk about guns and loads and dogs, and near-miss spills in open boats on the high seas, and I like the chance to get with others who enjoy these things.

But most of all, I like the work that this organization does. Providing and protecting the habitat in which ducks can nest is what DU does so well, and a more dedicated group of volunteers never was assembled.

Similar state organizations are springing all over the place. Their aim, usually, is to improve the conditions for waterfowl within that state's boundaries by acquiring, developing and helping to manage wetlands for the resident populations of ducks and geese and for the migrants that pass through each spring and fall. They exist by the contributions of the members who donate time, work, money and merchandise to the cause. In some states, the groups represent a formidable voting and lobbying bloc that lawmakers have to contend with. Bless 'em.

These organizations will sometimes sponsor an art contest that will feature a waterfowl stamp/print program. Duck stamps are an art form themselves, and the Federal Duck Stamp (Migratory Waterfowl Stamp) program is the granddaddy of them all. Numbered but not signed submissions are made, along with entrance fees, to the Interior Department. A group of judges is chosen, and the round of judging then begins. The actual judging takes many hours. For the artists, the work they submit is the work of a lifetime and reflects years of study, practice and courage.

Finally, a winner is chosen, the stamp is struck from the painting, and it is sold the next season to all waterfowlers.

The other half of the story is the collectible part. The collecting of Federal Duck Stamps, for example, is a passion with many. A friend of mine, stamp collector Harry Pittard, tells me that migratory stamps can range in value from a buck and a quarter to nearly $400, depending upon the year they were issued and whether they spent their lives in a stamp envelope untouched by human hands or riding around in your hip pocket with your name scrawled across them. In any event, it's nice to think about saving your own stamps—both the federal and state stamps, if your state issues them. They're a nice record of your past.

Art lovers really get into the prints for these stamps, too. The winning artist of the Federal Duck Stamp program, as part of the deal, has the right to market prints of the winning painting—and a gallery that has been lucky enough to sign the artist before or immediately after he or she has won stands to make some heavy money.

The money to the artist is big, too, as in the case of Bill Morris of Mobile, Alabama, the winner of the 1984-85 contest. His winning watercolor, "Widgeon," will be marketed as a piece of art. Prints from his original—25,000 to 30,000 of them—will be sold for about $135 each. In this regard, there are very few contests except your odd lottery here and there that can make the winner so immediately wealthy. Past winners say that they net between $1 and $2 million dollars from the sale of prints.

And, unlike a lottery which is a one-time deal, the work of the winning artist immediately increases in value once he's won. This includes both the work he will produce the rest of his life, as well as the work he's already done and sold plus remarques. It's like a lightning strike.

Sporting literature has always been devoted heavily to the waterfowling sports. Perhaps few wrote as eloquently about the subject as Nash Buckingham, the insurance man with the flair for the outdoors. His works are almost priceless to those who have them. Waterfowling literature in general is normally well accepted, but the old volumes, with their tales of long-ago times, big bags and bigger-than-life gunners, are among the best.

Right now there seems to be a renaissance in sporting literature. I think the reason is twofold. First, I think Americans are becoming more aware of the experiences that only good books can bring to them, and, secondly, I think that the vicarious experiences of those writers make us all a little richer. With old sporting literature, we can take a trip into the past and enjoy the hunts and bags that would get you a decade or two in the incarcetorium if you pulled it off today.

One other area that I predict will become a popular form of what we could call the "working collectible" is the refurbishing and use of fowling pieces from the past: old guns brought back to life.

With the advent of the smokeless powders years ago, the days of the twist-steel Damascus-barreled guns were numbered. Some of the finest examples of the gunmaker's art are now unsafe to shoot, and so they hang over someone's mantle. The balance, the feel, the style of these guns is unequaled in the eyes of many because they, too, tell of the bygone days.

But progress marches on, and with it improvements in the technology that can make these guns shootable again. Some have discovered that a titanium sleeve, fitted full length down the barrel of a 10-gauge fowling piece and then rebored for 12-gauge, makes an excellent blending of the old and the new. Unnoticeable from the outside, except at the muzzle, these sleeves put those old dandies back into our hands. Somehow, they would not seem fitting anywhere except in a duck blind.

Many an old gun will see a rebirth as this technology becomes more widespread, and the price of these previously-unshootable pieces will escalate as a result. To those who have Grampa's old smoothbore kicking around, why not give this a try?

Part of the "etcetera" of waterfowl hunting includes the sports involving the birds that are really part of waterfowling, but rarely thought of in that way.

Among these are the snipe and rails. These birds offer good sport; superb might be a better description of snipe shooting. Snipe at one time were a real delicacy to the tummies of Eastern epicures. Market gunners fashioned snipe decoys, along with those for curlews, now long since passed from the sporting scene. But the snipe persists, and is a challenging gamebird.

Snipe are migratory and inhabit the flats along rivers, lakes and coastal floodplains. Resembling undernourished woodcocks, they have a twisting flight that makes them tough as hell to hit with any consistency. At times, duck hunters have all seen a squadron of snipe buzzing their decoys, and goose hunters on the tundra often push clouds of the birds into the air as they make their way to the blinds, especially during September in the high latitudes.

Snipe are best hunted by a pair of shooters and a good retriever. Making a zig-zag pattern as they walk, they push snipe into the air. The trick with these birds is to wait until they quit juking you in flight and steady out. Often, they will swing over-head to get a better look at you, I guess, and high, overhead passing shots are the rule when this happens.

Shooting snipe takes fine shot—9s are great—and this makes the game tough in steel-shot-only areas, because steel doesn't come that small. It also takes fairly tight chokes because ranges tend toward being long, and a bird this small can slip through a loose pattern. So, we have a problem: A wildly jinking bird means large pattern spread to compensate, but a large pattern is ineffective at long ranges on a small bird. Hmmmmmm. It's best to stick with a modified barrel and fine shot and pass up anything past 35 yards.

Rail hunting is one waterfowl sport that most shooters have never been exposed to. Rail shooting—with Virginaias and soras the main staples—is best accomplished by two men working together, one pushing a flat-bottomed boat through reeds and the other handling the gunning. Unless you hire a pusher, you'll have to take your turn.

Rails sort of lumber into the air, and as a target are about as difficult as toy balloons wafting on a summer breeze. The challenge is to find them after they've been killed, and waiting until you are sure you won't tear up the meat before shooting. The rails I've shot didn't take a lot of killing, and I've often thought that a .410 would be fun. But since I regard this gauge as useful for skeet only—and maybe starlings in the barn—I've never tried it.

Another way to hunt rails is to have a couple of guys march through the marsh with a rope tied to their waists and tin cans with stones in them strung behind them. The noise of the cans flushes any nearby birds, and up they come. Here, the challenge comes in staying alive, because rail hunting is typically a September sport—late summer in the marsh—and it's damned hot.

Part of the lure of rail hunting is the fact that the bag limits are liberal—up to 15 birds in some areas—and also because the season generally opens earlier than other waterfowl seasons. By the way, a rail can compress its chest so that it can dart among the reeds on foot and not disturb the vegetation and thus tip off a predator about its whereabouts, hence, "Skinny as a rail." There's your piece of trivia for the day.

For those of us who do it, keeping a personal log or shooting diary can be a pleasant and enlightening experience. These logs are available commercially, or you can just take a loose-leaf notebook and keep the records you want in them.

My duck diary records the following data: date of hunt, names of companions, place we hunted, method (blind, floating, jump shooting, etc.), weather conditons (wind, cloud cover, precipitation, temperature, air pressure), species taken, number and type of decoys, and my personal shooting record.

This personal record documents the number of birds I shot at, the number I killed, their species, and what type of shot it was (incomer, quartering away right, quartering away left, passing through left to right or right to left). This way, I keep a regular tally of how lousy a shot I am; at least it gives me an excuse to drink.

But the log itself can be enlightening, because if you keep track of such things, it can tell you which of your hunting spots becomes productive at certain times of the year. For instance, there is one little, slow-moving river that is blue murder for floating about the third week of the season. The native ducks on nearby waters have usually been well-educated by this time, and the big fronts that move birds down out of Canada haven't materialized yet, so the birds head here to rest and hide. I go get them.

I know I keep coming back to this, but I'm going to again: Waterfowl hunting is, in its final form, recreation.

Since that's the case, and few of us—luckily—have to live off what we shoot, I'd like to offer to you some suggestions for making waterfowling even more fun when you can throw in some of the niceties that will spice up a day/trip/season.

First is the planning of an out-of-state or out-of-country hunt. Now, for some reasons I'll get to in the chapter called "The Future of the Sport," I'm not much inclined toward hunting waterfowl in Mexico or anywhere else on the wintering grounds. But for an out-of-country experience, a trip to Canada rivals, almost, an out-of-body experience.

There are problems that the first-timer should be aware of lest he fall prey to them, however. There is always some degree of difficulty in getting a firearm first into another country, and then getting it back into the United States. With the proper licenses and permits, obtained ahead of time, the hassle is knocked back to slightly intolerable, but be ready.

You're also best off to take the gun up without ammunition. You can amost always get what you want once you're on the other side of the border, but taking the gun and the shells with you usually proves a problem. After all, one hunter with a few boxes of birdshot *is* a threat to national security, right? You'll have fewer holdups in Customs if you don't have ammunition with you.

You should arrange ahead of time for a guide or at least a friendly Prairie farmer to help you along once you get there. Not just in waterfowling, but in any trip to new country many miles from home, a guide is an inexpensive investment compared with days wasted trying to figure things out. When you have a choice of spending time or money, spend the money; you can always earn more, but there's only so much time. Nothing is worse than figuring out the best way or place to hunt on the last day of your long-awaited trip, instead of the first day.

Getting a dog across the border is a matter of proper medical records, shot records, proper licensing papers and all the rest. If you can bear it, leave your dog at home if the guide has one. It will save time going and coming.

One nice thing about a Canadian Prairie trip is the opportunity to hunt some exotic, to many Easterners, upland birds. Prairie chickens, sharptail grouse and Hungarian partridge are some species that come to mind, and many parts of the Canadian plains have good pheasant shooting or pockets of really good ruffed grouse hunting as well.

Since hunting is recreation, why not sample as many forms as possible? Spending the morning and evening hours waterfowling and the middle of the day upland hunting is a great way to spend a trip. For this type of hunt, a gun with a variable choke or screw-in choke tubes is the ticket because it prevents having to bring a duck gun *and* and upland gun across the border.

A trip to the American prairies can be almost as much fun as a trip to Canada, without so much hassle or expense. Here, your Federal Duck Stamp is good with a nonresident license, and ducks are often overlooked on the plains.

One fun way to go about such a trip is to plan on camping when you go. Several hunters and a travel trailer can usually find a public area to set up shop, and the hunting, arranged ahead of time, can be superb in the corn and wheat stubble. Spicing up the middle of the day by going after pheasant or prairie grouse is just as possible here as it is in Canada. Contact the chamber of commerce or the state game department for help with guides and accommodations.

If you do make a trip like this, or elect to head north, consider taking a camera, either a good 35mm still camera or an 8mm home movie unit. Little adds more to the enjoyment of a trip or a season than a record of it, and few records are better than those kept on film. I like watching home movies of duck hunting. Most of the ones I've seen are amateurish at best, but they're still fun, and slides shown before the season to a flock of pals are guaranteed to get the collective blood boiling.

I'd suggest the still camera before I would the movies, however. There are many good cameras on the market that feature automatic settings of one type or another. So you don't have to be a genius to take good, crisp photos. Personally, I prefer a totally manual camera, or at least an automatic camera with a manual-override feature. This allows me to cope with situations when there may not be enough light for a shot, or when the shutter speed may have to be slow to use the available light, and then the action is blurred. Most of the professional photographers that I deal with in my work use manual cameras, so there must be a reason for it.

However, that's just my opinion. You may want the waterfowl photos you take to be shots of people or a dog making a nice retrieve or buddies packing up at the end of the day. If so, then consider an automatic camera. You may not even have to have a single-lens reflex camera; depending on your needs, a through-the-viewfinder model may be just as good. I'd also suggest that you shoot color slide film in ASA 64: It gives good resolution, fine prints can be made from it, the slides are fun to show on a screen, and that speed film is very flexible in differing light conditions.

10

Duck Camp

If you haven't chopped up this book and used it to start a fire in your pot-bellied stove yet, then you remember the opening segment about what it was like in the old days, when we captains of industry got together at our exclusive ducking club to lay waste to the canvasbacks that filled the skies.

A return to those days is something all of us would like, even if just for a while, but what I'm going to suggest is the next best thing to it: the creation of a duck or goose hunting club.

Forming such an association means an investment in money, time and brain power. It also takes a plan, and knowing what you want beforehand is critical.

First, in some parts of the country leases are a way of life, especially in the Southwest where little public hunting land exists. But in other parts of the country, land near a refuge or on some major waterfowl flyway is usually available for renting or buying. Here is where your investigations should begin. Not much land is needed; actually, as little as 80 good acres can make a fine club. More is better, of course, because it gives you a chance to have several types of preferred habitats in one parcel of land.

Some clubs simply consist of pit blinds in harvested fields that the birds visit morning and evening. Others have shoreline with deepwater blinds for diving ducks, flooded woods, cropfields, you name it.

Once you've found the land you want, then the negotiations with the owner begin. Several dollars an acre or more is about the going rate in the Midwest—more on the Coasts. Some marginal areas can be leased for the taxes, but don't count on it. What you want to determine is the cost, because then you will have to go out and recruit members to split those costs. If a club's land can be leased for, say, $3000 a year, three of you can pony up a grand each and enjoy. Or, six of you can part with $500 and enjoy half as much. Because the number of hunters will become unwieldy at some point, you'll want to get a piece of land that's affordable so that the number of participants can be kept down and the shooting opportunities can be kept up.

Let me speak from some hard-won experience here: Be very careful who you ask to join your club. Make sure that there will be a blending of personalities that will enhance the experience and that people who are brought in are known to all the members and are on good terms. If four of you get together to form a club, make sure you resemble Porthos, Athos, Aramis and D'artanigan—all for one and one for all. If the four of you are made up of two pairs of buddies, then you've got the potential makings of cliques, which will ruin everything. Also remember: "Men trifle with their politics, and they trifle with their careers, but they don't trifle with their sport."

There is a fine line between costs and the number of members it will take to cover those costs; too much money equals too many members, and there isn't enough space or time for all to get their money's worth out of it.

When picking the members, also remember that work schedules are important. One happy club I know of runs well because the membership consists of two policemen who work weekends but have days off during the week, a traditional nine-to-fiver with Saturdays and Sundays to hunt, and a plant superintendent who works the second shift and can hunt any morning he wishes. Cute.

Once you've found the area you want and the negotiations and membership planning are well underway, make sure that the deal you cut with the landowner is iron-clad. You'll have to know his farming plans, if any, you'll want the lease to have a renewable option after the first year (you may have to sweeten the pot to get this rider attached), and you'll want to make sure that you have exclusive use of the area for hunting. I know some fellows who took the waterfowling rights to a place for a song only to discover, later, that the same farmer had sold the deer hunting rights to another group—talk about a fiasco.

Naturally, get this all in writing, and if you have a pal who's an attorney, get him to draw up a paper and get it witnessed and notarized; it's the safest way and nobody, these days, should be insulted. Above all, beware of the guy who says, "I don't believe in them there contracts—just gimme your hand on it." Believe me, he'll mess with you.

An alternative to leasing land is to buy it outright instead. This works best if the land is a marsh or is in some way unusable to a farmer. It's best to lease it for a couple of years, kick in a few extra dollars, and get an "option to buy" clause written in, with part of the leasing fee applicable toward the purchase price, say 25 cents on the dollar. Now, if you own land, is when the fun starts. But I urge you not to buy land right off because the membership can change or you may find the ducks aren't using the area like you figured they would. You can always wait for a lease to expire; it's tougher if you own the place.

What I'm going to say about having a spot for keeps can also be said if you have a long-term lease and the owner doesn't object. I'd say the nicest arrangement is when you're able to place some permanent buildings on the property, such as a clubhouse/sleeping quarters, a shed for decoys, boats and assorted gear, and a kennel. These can usually be constructed for a lot less money than you'd think, because the labor is free and you can put up with a lot fewer of the creature comforts at duck camp than you would at home.

Here is a good chance to choose your membership so that the skills it will take to organize and construct a working camp are represented among your cronies. If you know a good duck hunter who's a fine companion and a good sport who also happens to be a carpenter, well . . .

Once the membership is assembled, it's time to put personal feelings aside and sit down and talk. By this I mean you've got to get the division of labor out of the way, and you've got to be sure that all parties understand that they'll have to work at making this a good camp. Firewood has to be cut, decoys and boats have to be painted, blinds have to be constructed, pits dug, buildings put up, dishes washed, etcetera. If the same few guys do it all while the rest are out hunting, bad feelings are going to surface like dead carp. Write down what all the chores are and how the rotation is going to take place so that all hands get a turn at the hard stuff.

If there is a major project, such as house painting, schedule it so everybody can be there, and don't do it until everybody *is* there. Otherwise, there will always be "business considerations" that will take a member away at the critical time.

Make sure that all understand the time for the payment of their part of the lease, and get that in writing as well. We all have bills and fiscal responsibilities, but the members should come in with a clear eye and cool head and no false expectations about what a pittance it will cost them to go ducking in style. Tell them the date that they have to pay their share of the lease or purchase payment, and that they have to be accountable for it. There can be no "carrying" someone, because that's when tempers can really get ragged. I've seen members carried for two years at small clubs, and it places a real hardship on the others. Demand the money by a certain date, and if someone is 30 days in arrears, he's out.

I know this sounds hard-hearted, but hunting is supposed to be fun. If there are nagging doubts among the members about one person who is always late with his share of the money or work, better to, as the Bible says, "cut off that hand" and be done with it. There will be some hard feelings at first, but nothing like there will be later if the problem persists. The *last* thing you need at camp is a fistfight.

If you own the land or have a good lease arrangement, there's no reason why families can't be included in the festivities. Opening day at some camps is like Christmas, and everyone from neighboring leases drops in to visit, sign the camp guest book, and tip a Nehi while they lie through their teeth about their shooting. Families can be included in summer picnics, blind building or maybe some fishing if your land contains that option. The more that wives and kids understand about duck camp, the more they'll approve—probably. Well, maybe.

Also, set down in writing the rules about guests. Some clubs have a very succinct rule: No guests, period. Others take into consideration the family members, although this can cause problems. Let's say that Member A has no children, while Member B has two teenaged sons. If family members are given carte blanche to come and go, then B is getting three times what A is getting in terms of use from the land.

Other members may have a lot of pals, and such members almost always show up at camp on Friday night with one or two cronies in town for the weekend. It makes the other, paying members a little tight in the jaw.

In this regard, I think you have to make sure that all get use of the land exclusively from time to time. If your days off are Wednesday and Thursday, and nobody else can get away on those days, then you should be allowed to bring a specified number of guests to the club during the season on those days. If you all have only the weekends off, however, then there should be no guests. Some clubs with members who work Monday to Friday get around this by using vacation time from work during the gunning season.

Whatever you work out, you should make sure that, time-wise, the following arrangements are made: time you will all be at the club together; time you will each have the club to yourselves, privately; when guests will be allowed, if at all, and the number of times you can bring guests (private time or "common" time); and, will hunting-aged children automatically become members?

The discussion of equipment is also something that should be worked out ahead of time. Some duck hunters have been collecting gear for years, and can bring a lot of it to camp. Others, no less enthusiastic, have been at it a short time and their list of equipment gets a little sketchy after a gun and a pair of waders. I think it works best if all members pool their equipment and use it as common property, guns, shotshells and dogs aside.

The reason I say this is because it is better to find members with whom you will want to share your stuff, rather than worrying about, "Who had my boat this afternoon?" and other such things. If the camp is going to work, it has to be based upon mutual trust and sharing. Keeping track of "my stuff and your stuff" gets to be a pain.

Likewise, any major purchases, such as new boats, should be joint ventures. Someone once said of his children, "I have two children by natural birth, and two by adoption, but I can never remember which are which." This is the way to think about camp equipment. You can always sort it out later if the camp breaks up. Better to go in with the idea that this will be a permanent venture.

Occasionally, for reasons beyond his control, a member has to pull out. Sickness, loss of income or job transfer can take a member away, so provisions on how this will be handled should be made in writing. One of the best ways to deal with this situation is to have the departing member try to make arrangements for his place to be taken by another who is acceptable to the originals. Or, the other members can decide to absorb that member's share of the costs and work against the time when he can rejoin. Or, they just may decide to drop the number of members by one and not replace him. Whatever you decide to do, get it in writing *before* it happens.

Here, then, is a list of Do's for making a duck camp work:

DO make sure that all members share equally in the work.

DO make sure that all members pay in full and promptly; do not accept donations of equipment to the camp in lieu of payment.

DO make sure that all members get use of the club privately at least once during the season.

DO make sure that all members get equal chance at the best blinds or shooting locations.

DO make sure that you have a policy on guests and family members using the club.

DO make sure that your lease gives you exclusivity, even if you have to pay more.

DO make sure that you have an option to buy if at all possible.

DO make sure that you have a one-year trial, and then re-evaluate before entering into a long-term agreement.

DO make sure that you have a policy concerning a member's pulling out.

DO make sure that all parties are philosophically in line with one another regarding the sport of waterfowling.

DO make sure that equipment, aside from personal items, is community property.

11

The Future of
the Sport

Was a time, not too long ago, when we were, as I've mentioned
before, a nation of waterfowlers. Not so today, sad to say.

Upland hunting is now what waterfowling once was, and
the burgeoning deer populations have made every man a big-
game hunter. The waterfowler is in a decline. To give you an
idea, take a look at the drop in sales of Federal Duck Stamps in
three Midwest states according, to the Fish and Wildlife Service
(attached Table No. 1).

The number of waterfowlers is dropping like a head-shot
mallard, and, frankly, it's got the F & A boys in a quandary.

Further, there are rumblings out of Canada that the numbers
of returning waterfowl are not what they should be. In particular,
there is a noticeable decline in the number of nesting black ducks

Table 1. Fish and Wildlife Duck Service Stamp Sales

	Indiana	*Ohio*	*Michigan*
1973	25,398	36,994	103,886
1974	26,280	40,064	104,805
1975	24,016	41,819	103,893
1976	15,939	41,823	84,745
1977	15,215	38,412	72,096
1978	15,364	39,483	65,055
1979	15,757	37,833	62,187
1980	15,073	36,162	56,495
1981	14,965	34,687	49,261
1982*	14,035	28,568	48,565
% Decrease 1975–1982	−42%	−33%	−53%

*Preliminary sales figures

on and along the East Coast, leading to special hunting restrictions on this species as the mid- 1980's approach. (Recent findings show Black ducks are blatantly breeding with mallards over much of their range, however, so the decline in the species may not reflect a decline in the number of ducks *per se*.) Some species of brant are also doing poorly, perhaps due to predation by man on their nesting grounds.

Possibly the best way to determine why the number of waterfowlers is dropping off is to take a look at a rather well-done scientific study carried out by Charles Nelson, a pal, and David Feltus and David Safronoff, all from Michigan State University. They did some in-depth sampling of hunter attitudes and divided the groups into hunters (present and active) and "dropouts," those who call themselves former waterfowl hunters.

Their findings are recorded here, thanks to their permission, and although the study was done in Michigan, I think you will agree that the reasons are pretty basic, regardless of the area of the country.

I also think it's safe to assume that the days of the big bag limits are gone, and that there are a number of restrictions which foster a persecution complex in some waterfowlers: steel shot in some areas, Federal Migratory Stamps, state migratory stamps, a smattering of day-use fees, limits to the number of shells you can take with you in some areas, boat registrations, enough safety cushions for all passengers, ad infinitum. Objections to these restrictions, compared with the relatively few restrictions on upland hunters, for example, have turned some of the waterfowl fraternity into pheasant hunters.

Further, as the tables indicate, there is almost a synergism of factors that have made some waterfowlers drop the sport: high costs for shells, stamps, decoys, boats and all the related paraphernalia; availability of hunting areas; the decorum—or lack of it—by other hunters; too little reward for too much work, and so forth.

From this report, I'm going to quote, with the permission of the Michigan State researchers:

Socio-Economic Characteristics

"Duck hunters have a slightly higher average income than dropouts. About half of both groups have annual family incomes in excess of $24,999 (Table 2). This is somewhat higher than the 1980 census estimate of $22,108 for Michigan median family income."

Geese—a waterfowl management success story. Nesting too far north to be disturbed and aided by a refuge system second to none, the numbers of Canadas in North America have been on the increase so that, in parts of the country, the birds are actually a nuisance. Photo by Steven Griffin.

Table 2. 1981 Household Family Income for Hunters and Dropouts

Annual Household Family Income	Dropouts N–372	Hunters N–448
	——— Percent ———	
10,000	9.7*	4.9
10–14,999	14.2	11.2
15–19,999	12.9	12.1
20–24,999	13.7	17.6
25–29,999	14.0	11.4
30–34,999	10.8	14.0
35–39,999	7.3	10.0
40–44,999	5.9	6.5
45–50,000	3.5	4.9
50,000	8.1	7.4
Mean Income**	26,900*	28,900

*Significant difference between dropouts and hunters p ≤ .05.
**Calculated using grouped date techniques and a maximum income of $75,000. Results rounded to nearest $100.

"Statewide, both duck hunters and dropouts average about 37 years of age (Table 3). Duck hunters and dropouts outside of Region III (densely populated) average around 40 years of age. Five years should be subtracted from these averages to estimate the average age of waterfowl hunters in 1977. If recruitment and dropout patterns have remained constant, this adjusted average

Table 3. Age of Hunters and Dropouts in 1981

Age	Dropouts N–400	Hunters N–475
	——— Percent** ———	
11–20	5.8	6.5
21–30	33.3*	26.3
31–40	26.5	30.5
41–50	14.8	18.9
51–60	13.3	11.4
61–70	5.0	5.5
71–80	1.3	0.8
Mean Age	37.1	37.8

*Significant difference between dropouts and hunters p ≤ .05.
**Percents may not add to 100 due to rounding.

Table 4. Education Levels of Hunters and Dropouts

Education	Dropouts N–398	Hunters N–476
	Percent**	
Less than high school	9.3	8.8
High school	48.0*	39.3
Some college	26.4	29.4
College degree	7.5	11.1
Graduate school	8.8	11.3
Mean Education	13.1*	13.5

*Significant difference between dropouts and hunters p ≤ .05.
**Percents may not add to 100 due to rounding.

could serve as an estimate of the average age of waterfowl hunters in 1982.

"On the average, duck hunters have somewhat more education than dropouts. Slightly more than 40% of dropouts and over 50% of duck hunters statewide have some college education (Table 4)."

"Of respondent waterfowl hunters and dropouts living in Michigan, 78% live in Region III (densely populated), 14% live in Region II (moderately populated), and 8% live in Region I (sparsely populated) (Table 5). Almost 60% live in counties which require steel shot (Table 6)."

Hunting Behavior

"Approximately 34% of all respondents used state managed waterfowl areas for 1 or more percent of their 1981 waterfowl hunting. About 20% of total waterfowl hunting time was spent

Table 5. Percent of Respondents by Region of Residence

DNR Planning Region	N	Dropouts N–384	Hunters N–467	Total N–851
		Percent		
Sparsely populated	68	3	5	8
Moderately populated	119	7	7	14
Densely populated	664	35	43	78
Total		45	55	100

Table 6. Percent of Respondents by Counties Requiring Steel Shot in 1981

County Type	Dropouts N = 384	Hunters N = 467	Total N = 851
	———— Percent ————		
Steel shot	26%	34%	60%
Non-steel shot	19%	21%	40%
Total	45%	55%	100%

on these areas (Table 7). Almost a quarter of steel shot zone hunting was on managed areas. In Region III (densely populated) hunters spent more time on managed areas than dropouts. This situation was reversed for Region II (Table 8)."

"Most waterfowl hunters did most of their hunting in the county they lived in. Over 75% of Region I (sparsely populated) hunters and dropouts hunted most in their residence county as did over half of those in Regions II and III (moderately populated, densely populated). Hunters in steel shot counties were more likely to do most of their waterfowl hunting in their residence county than hunters in non-steel shot counties."

"On the average both hunters and dropouts expended about 90% of their waterfowl hunting efforts in their favorite hunting

Table 7. Percent of Season Spent in Managed Areas

Percent of Season	Percent of Respondents	Cumulative Percent
0	66.0	66.0
1–10	6.4	72.4
11–20	2.7	75.1
21–30	3.4	78.5
31–40	1.5	80.2
41–50	2.2	82.4
51–60	.5	82.9
61–70	.6	83.5
71–80	3.0	86.5
81–90	3.1	89.6
91–100	10.4	100.0
Mean = 19.67%		

Table 8. Mean Percent of Time Spent in Managed Areas by Region

DNR Planning Region	N	Dropouts N–372	Hunters N–455	Total N–827
			Percent	
Sparsely populated	67	10.5	9.5	10.0
Moderately populated	111	21.5	13.7	17.3
Densely populated	649	19.2*	25.1	22.5

*Significant difference between dropouts and hunters p ≤ .05.

county, whether this was their residence county or some other county. Differences between regions were slight."

"Both dropouts and hunters tended to do the bulk of their hunting in October; hunters averaged about 67% and dropouts 73% (Table 9). Average percent of hunting in November for dropouts was 24% and for hunters 30%. December and January averages were less than 3% and reflect the restricted waterfowl hunting opportunities."

"Over time, more hunters and dropouts tended to hunt most with friends and alone and less with immediate family or other relatives (Table 10). For the last season hunted almost 70% of the respondents hunted waterfowl most with friends or alone."

"More than half the respondents hunted whatever was available rather than a specific type of duck or goose (Table 11). About a quarter of the respondents were puddle duck hunters and the rest were diving duck or goose hunters."

"Close to 50% of dropouts and close to 60% of hunters usually hunted from a blind during the last season they hunted (Table 12). Jump shooting was next most popular with about 20% of dropouts and 14% of hunters selecting it. Pass shooting

Table 9. Mean Percent of Hunting in Different Months for Hunters and Dropouts

Group	N	October	November	December	January
			Percent of hunting		
Dropouts	402	73.1*	23.9	1.6	.3
Hunters	482	66.9	30.1	2.1	.6

*Significant difference between hunters and dropouts p ≤ .05.

Table 10. Primary Hunting Companions in First and Last Year of Hunting

Primary Companions	First Year N = 890	Last Year N = 890
	Percent	
	Dropouts	Hunters
Immediate family	41.2*	24.9
Other relatives	7.8*	5.2
Friends	44.0*	56.0
Alone	7.0*	13.9

*Significant difference between dropouts and hunters p ≤ .05.

Table 11. Type of Waterfowl Hunted

Type	Dropouts N–407	Hunters N–467	Total N–874
		Percent**	
Puddle duck	24.3	30.0	27.4
Diving duck	6.1	8.4	7.4
Goose	12.5	13.4	13.0
Whatever available	57.1*	48.1	52.3

*Significant difference between dropouts and hunters p ≤ .05.
**Percents may not add to 100 due to rounding.

Table 12. Usual Method of Waterfowl Hunting

Method	Dropouts N = 407	Hunters N = 467	Total N = 874
		Percent**	
Blind	48.2*	59.1	54.0
Layout boat	2.0	3.4	2.7
Sneakboat	2.5	1.5	1.9
Jump shooting	19.2*	13.7	16.2
Pass shooting	14.3	11.6	12.8
Dry field	8.4	6.6	7.4
Floating river	5.7	4.1	4.8

*Significant difference between dropouts and hunters p ≤ .05.
**Percents may not add to 100 due to rounding.

Table 13. Age at Which Dropouts and Hunters First Hunted Waterfowl

Age	Dropouts N = 410	Hunters N = 480	Total N = 890
		Percent**	
<12	2.2	4.4	3.4
12–13	13.9	17.7	16.0
14–15	20.5	21.5	21.0
16–17	20.5	21.9	21.2
18–19	12.7	9.4	10.9
20–21	5.9	4.2	4.9
22+	24.3	20.9	22.6

*Significant difference between dropouts and hunters p ≤ .05.
**Percents may not add to 100 due to rounding.

is the only other hunting method which more than 10% of dropouts and hunters marked as their usual method.''

"More than half the dropouts had started hunting waterfowl by the time they were 18 and more than half the hunters by the time they were 16 (Table 13). About 20% of both groups started hunting waterfowl after they turned 22.''

"As might be expected dropouts averaged considerably fewer waterfowl seasons than hunters (Table 14). The most striking difference is in the range from 1 to 5 seasons. Over 40% of the

Table 14. Number of Seasons Hunted

Seasons Hunted	Dropouts N–407	Hunters N–480	Total N–887
		Percent**	
1–5	39.8*	9.8	23.6
6–10	22.3	26.4	24.6
11–15	13.3	17.1	15.3
16–20	7.6*	15.7	12.0
21–25	5.0*	10.4	8.0
26–30	4.2	7.1	5.7
31–60	7.1*	13.4	10.9
Mean Seasons	11.9*	17.6	15.0

*Significant difference between dropouts and hunters p ≤ .05.
**Percents may not add to 100 due to rounding.

dropouts had hunted 5 or fewer seasons while slightly less than 10% of the hunters had.''

"More than 55% of the dropouts hunted 5 or less times the last season they hunted (Table 15). In contrast, less than 25% of the hunters had hunted 5 times or less. More than half of the hunters hunted 10 or more times.''

"Respondents were asked to rank their three most important sources of information about waterfowl hunting. Other hunters were by far the most important single source (Table 16). Magazines, the Wildlife Division's Waterfowl Guide and newspapers were the three next most important sources of information.''

Complaints and Concerns

"Perhaps the most important portion of the questionnaire asked respondents to single out their one most important complaint or concern and to pick their one most important specific complaint or concern under that basic heading.''

"Regulations were chosen as the most important basic complaint by approximately 40% of both hunters and dropouts (Table 17). Generally differences between steel shot and non-steel shot counties were small (Table 18A, Table 18B). Regulations were singled out relatively more often by hunters in non-steel shot counties and relatively less often by dropouts in non-steel coun-

Table 15. Number of Times Hunted in Last Season

Times Hunted	Dropouts N = 407	Hunters N = 471	Total N = 878
		Percent**	
1–5	56.3*	24.5	39.3
6–10	26.5	30.4	28.6
11–15	9.5*	17.0	13.6
16–20	4.1*	12.6	8.6
21–25	0.9*	5.2	3.3
26 +	2.7*	10.3	6.6
Mean Days	7.1*	12.9	10.2

*Significant difference between dropouts and hunters p ≤ .05.
**Percents may not add to 100 due to rounding.

Table 16. Respondents' Three Most Important Sources of Hunting Information

Source	Most* Important	Second Most Important	Third Most Important	Total
Television	15	54	105	174
Radio	4	13	31	48
Newspaper	113	245	365	723
Other Hunters	212	366	510	1088
License Dealer	35	123	204	362
Waterfowl Guide	130	242	354	726
Magazines	165	278	366	809
DNR personnel	45	105	164	314
Sports Organization	39	85	123	247
FWS	6	37	80	123
Other	18	20	45	83

*The values in each column represent the number of respondents giving each source the indicated rank.

ties. Fifty or more percent of both hunters and dropouts in Region I felt regulations were the most important problem.''

"Cost was the second most frequently selected category overall. About 20% of all respondents selected it. Dropouts chose

Table 17. Proportions of Hunters and Dropouts Selecting Basic Complaints

Basic Complaint	Dropouts N–355	Hunters N–420	Overall N–775
	Percent**		
Waterfowl hunting regulations	39.7	45.0	42.6
Cost of waterfowl hunting	23.7*	17.9	20.5
No complaints or concerns	9.3	6.9	8.0
Other seasons conflict with waterfowl season	7.0*	3.3	5.0
Behavior of other waterfowl hunters	6.2*	10.5	8.5
Not enough ducks and/or geese	5.9	5.5	5.7
No good place to hunt waterfowl	5.6	3.8	4.6
DNR waterfowl hunting area management	1.4	3.3	2.5
Other complaint or concern	1.1*	3.8	2.6

*Significant difference between dropouts and hunters p ≤ .05.
**Percents may not add to 100 due to rounding.

Table 18A. Proportions of Hunters and Dropouts Living in *Steel Shot* Counties Selecting Basic Complaints

Basic Complaint	Dropouts N = 190	Hunters N = 247	Overall N = 437
	——— Percent** ———		
Waterfowl hunting regulations	43.7	42.1	42.8
Cost of waterfowl hunting	26.3	21.9	23.8
No complaints or concerns	4.7	5.7	5.3
Other seasons conflict with waterfowl season	3.7	3.2	3.4
Behavior of other waterfowl hunters	4.7*	10.1	7.8
Not enough ducks and/or geese	7.4	4.5	5.7
No good place to hunt waterfowl	6.8	4.0	5.3
DNR waterfowl hunting area management	1.1*	4.5	3.0
Other complaint or concern	1.6	4.0	3.0

*Significant difference between dropouts and hunters p ≤ .05.
** Column percents may not add to 100 due to rounding.

Table 18B. Proportions of Hunters and Dropouts Living in *Non-Steel Shot* Counties Selection Basic Complaints

Basic Complaint	Dropouts N = 136	Hunters N = 160	Overall N = 296
	——— Percent** ———		
Waterfowl hunting regulations	36.8*	49.4	43.6
Cost of waterfowl hunting	18.4	13.1	15.5
No complaints or concerns	12.5	7.5	9.8
Other seasons conflict with waterfowl season	12.5*	3.7	7.8
Behavior of other waterfowl hunters	8.8	11.9	10.5
Not enough ducks and/or geese	4.4	5.6	5.1
No good place to hunt waterfowl	4.4	3.7	4.1
DNR waterfowl hunting area management	1.5	1.9	1.7
Other complaint or concern	0.7	3.1	2.0

*Significant difference between dropouts and hunters p ≤ .05.
**Percents may not add to 100 due to rounding.

it slightly more frequently than hunters. It was also more important in steel shot than non-steel shot counties."

"For hunters, the behavior of other hunters tended to get the third highest proportion of responses. It was selected by over 10% of them. Dropout responses varied too much region to region and between steel shot and non-steel shot counties for a clear third most important category to emerge."

"Less than 7% of all respondents felt not enough ducks, no good place to hunt, or (wildlife agency) waterfowl hunting area management was their most important basic complaint or concern."

"In general, very few specific complaints were selected by as many as 4% of the respondents. Every specific category under the regulations heading was selected by at least 4% of hunters or dropouts."

"Steel shot and poor season dates are indicated most frequently by hunters statewide (Table 19) and in steel shot counties

Table 19. Specific Complaints Selected by More Than 4% of Hunters or Dropouts

Specific Complaint	Dropouts N–355	Hunters N–420	Overall N–775
	——— Percent*** ———		
Regulations			
Steel shot is unnecessary	9.3	10.1	9.8
Too many regulations	7.3	7.2	7.3
Bag limit is too low	5.8	5.1	5.4
Poor season dates	4.7*	11.6	8.4
Too many licenses	4.4	2.4	3.3
Point system too complicated	4.4*	1.4	2.8
Shooting hours aren't long enough	1.7*	5.3	3.7
Costs			
Duck stamp cost	11.6*	7.0	9.1
Steel shot cost	4.4	6.5	5.5
Competing Activities	3.5	1.7	2.5
Hunter Behaviors			
Sky shooting	2.6	4.3	3.6

*Significant differences between dropouts and hunters p ≤ .05.
**Category included if 4% was exceeded by any subgroup of respondents.
***Column percents do not add to 100 because not all categories were included.

(Table 20A). Dropouts complained most frequently about steel shot and duck stamp costs."

"In counties where steel shot is required, poor season dates and steel shot again received the highest proportions of complaints (Table 20B). Dropouts selected duck stamp cost and poor season dates more often than any other specific complaints."

A much higher proportion of dropouts in non-steel shot counties than hunters felt that the season conflict between waterfowl and archery deer was their most important specific complaint."

Who Dropped Out

"We also looked at what proportions of which groups of respondents dropped out. The overall dropout rate was 46%. Many subgroups had higher or lower dropout rates."

Table 20A. Specific Complaints Selected by More Than 4% of Hunters or Dropouts for Respondents Living in Steel Shot Counties**

Specific Complaint	Dropouts N-183	Hunters N-244	Overall N-427
	———— Percent*** ————		
Regulations			
Steel shot is unnecessary	14.2	10.7	12.2
Too many regulations	8.2	7.0	7.5
Bag limit is too low	5.5	3.7	4.4
Poor season dates	3.3*	11.1	7.7
Too many licenses	3.3	2.0	2.6
Point system too complicated	4.4	1.2	2.6
Shooting hours aren't long enough	2.2	4.1	3.3
Costs			
Duck stamp cost	12.6	7.8	9.8
Steel shot cost	6.6	9.0	8.0
Competing Activities			
Archery deer hunting	2.2	1.6	1.9
Hunter Behaviors			
Sky shooting	2.7	4.9	4.0

*Significant difference between dropouts and hunters p ≤ .05.
**Category included if 4% was exceeded by any subgroup of respondents.
***Column percents do not add to 100 because not all categories were included.

Table 20B. Specific Complaints Selected by More Than 4% of Hunters or Dropouts for Respondents Living in Non-Steel Shot Counties**

Specific Complaint	Dropouts N-132	Hunters N-157	Overall N-289
	——— Percent*** ———		
Regulations			
Steel shot is unnecessary	3.8	8.3	6.2
Too many regulations	5.3	7.0	6.2
Bag limit is too low	6.8	7.6	7.3
Poor season dates	7.6	12.7	10.4
Too many licenses	3.3	2.0	2.6
Point system too complicated	4.5	1.9	3.1
Shooting hours aren't long enough	1.5*	7.6	4.8
Costs			
Duck stamp cost	10.6	6.4	8.3
Steel shot cost	2.3	3.2	2.8
Competing Activities			
Archery deer hunting	6.1	1.9	3.8
Hunter Behaviors			
Sky shooting	3.0	3.8	3.5

*Significant difference between dropouts and hunters p ≤ .05.
**Category included if 4% was exceeded by any subgroup of respondents.
***Column percents do not add to 100 because not all categories were included.

"Respondents who have hunted 16 or more seasons have dropout rates considerably lower than 46% as do those who hunted 11 or more times the last season they hunted. Those who hunted only 1 or 2 seasons had a 78% dropout rate. Respondents who hunted 1 to 2 times during the last season had a 66% dropout rate."

"Of those respondents who adopted waterfowl hunting between the ages of 20 and 24, 58% dropped out. The dropout rate for hunters who hunt whatever waterfowl are available was 50% (Table 21). When respondents who hunt waterfowl primarily from a blind are compared to respondents who use all other methods, they have a significantly lower dropout rate (Table 22). The small number of respondents who hunt from layout boats prevents the seemingly large difference between their dropout rate and that of respondents who use other methods from being

Table 21. Type of Waterfowl Hunted by Dropout Rate

Type Hunted	N	Percent Dropped Out
Puddle Duck	242	41
Diving Duck	65	38
Goose	115	44
Whatever Available	462	50

statistically significant. Respondents who spend 61% to 80% of their waterfowl hunting effort on managed areas have a dropout rate of only 16% (Table 23).''

"While proportions dropping out for various basic complaint categories appear to be different, none of the differences were significant at $p \leq .05$. (Table 24). This is also true for specific complaint categories (Table 25).''

I'd like to make a few comments of my own regarding the data highlighted by the Michigan State University study. Obviously, waterfowl hunting is an expensive sport. The investment in equipment is high when compared with other forms of shooting, and this is reflected in the income rates/dropout rates shown in Table 2.

And, the fact that the biggest share of the dropouts was in the 21–30 age category (Table 3) is perhaps a function of this income factor: those are the ages when hunters, and Americans in general, are on their own financially and at their lowest income earning levels because they are just entering the job market.

Table 22. Preferred Hunting Method by Dropout Rate

Hunting Method	N	Percent Dropped Out
Blind	472	41
Layout boat	24	33
Sneakboat	17	59
Jump shooting	142	55
Pass shooting	112	52
Dry field	65	52
Floating river	23	55

Table 23. Percent of Season Spent on Managed Areas by Dropout Rate

Percent of Hunting	N	Percent Dropped Out
0–20	684	48
21–40	45	40
41–60	25	36
61–80	32	16
81–100	120	47

Table 3 shows that the biggest glut of active hunters is in the 31–40 age group, when finances may not be that big a problem anymore.

Table 4 shows that even though the mean education levels are within four months of one another for hunters and dropouts, there are more active hunters with educations beyond high school. Again, this could be a related financial factor because the higher education level for active shooters probably manifests itself in a higher average income.

Table 9 deals with the months that hunters and dropouts do—or did—most of their hunting, and shows pretty clearly that the active waterfowlers were more likely to hunt longer into the year than the dropouts, a measure of dedication as anyone who has sat through a November gale can attest to.

Table 11 tends to back this up. It shows that the dropouts

Table 24. Basic Complaints by Dropout Rate

Basic Complaint	N	Percent Dropped Out
Waterfowl hunting regulations	330	43
Cost of waterfowl hunting	159	53
No complaints or concerns	62	53
Other seasons conflict with waterfowl season	39	64
Behavior of other waterfowl hunters	66	33
Not enough ducks and/or geese	44	48
No good place to hunt waterfowl	36	56
DNR waterfowl hunting area management	19	26
Other complaint or concern	20	20

Table 25. Specific Complaints by Dropout Rate

Specific Complaint	N	Percent Dropped Out
Regulations		
Steel shot is unnecessary	74	43
Too many regulations	55	46
Bag limit is too low	41	49
Poor season dates	64	25
Too many licenses	25	60
Point system too complicated	21	71
Shooting hours aren't long enough	28	21
Costs		
Duck stamp cost	69	58
Steel shot cost	42	36
Competing Activities		
Archery deer hunting	19	63
Hunter Behaviors		
Sky shooting	27	33

were more likely to be "grabbag" hunters as opposed to specialists. The dropouts tended to hunt what was available, which means that they probably had less knowledge of what it took to go after a specific waterfowl type—goose, diving duck, puddle duck.

Table 12 points out something interesting as well. Most of those hunters who are active waterfowlers are likely to do their hunting from a blind—more than the dropouts. There is also a pretty large difference in the number of dropouts who did their waterfowling by jump shooting and pass shooting when compared with the hunters.

This may well be because the hunters possess the skill and the equipment to do their hunting over decoys. Here, I'm talking about boats, decoys, calls and calling, dogs—all the things that take time, experience and money to accumulate and learn to use. Jump shooting and pass shooting are examples of waterfowling of the "bare bones" variety: they're more like upland hunting because they're more catch-as-catch-can and more dependent upon luck than skill, as blind hunting is. This is not meant to denigrate these forms of hunting, of course.

Table 13, as indicated earlier, also shows that the hunters started at a younger age than did the dropouts. This is good data for such youth-oriented programs as Duck Unlimited's *Greenwing* program for young hunters. The fact of the matter is, if you get kids interested early, they are more likely to stay with hunting than if they came into the sport relatively late in life.

And, the hunters are more likely to have hunted longer, probably owing to their comparatively early start in the sport (Table 14). Most of the dropouts, more than 60 percent, hunted less than 10 years, while of the active waterfowlers, about 60 percent have hunted *longer* than 10 years.

Besides starting younger, having hunted longer, and therefore having more experience, the hunters who called themselves active hunt more each season than the dropouts did the last year they hunted before quitting the sport.

Table 15 shows that the dropouts hunted far fewer days in their last season than did the hunters—7.1 as opposed to almost 13 days, respectively. Among the hunters, there is a core of more than 10 percent who hunted in excess of 26 days a year—and their wives thought they were working overtime!

Table 16 shows that the word-of-mouth network is alive and well among waterfowlers. "Other hunters" were the most-often quoted source of information among the respondents. In my experience, there is a real hotline among dedicated shooters in each waterfowling community. Near any public refuge where open hunting is allowed, the word gets out pretty quickly which areas on the grounds are producing. I know that on the night before a hunt, I get on the phone to several of my friends who are avid duck hunters and start pumping them about who's taking what and where. It works.

Table 17 showed some things about the attitudes of waterfowlers, especially where their complaints were concerned. More hunters than dropouts cited waterfowl hunting regulations as a problem worth griping about, which is interesting. Probably because they've been hunting longer and hunt more, the active hunters were more likely to have run afoul of changes in seasons lengths, shooting times and bag limits.

As indicated elsewhere, the dropouts were more inclined than the hunters to cite the expense of waterfowling as a problem area.

One fascinating aspect was the fact that the dropouts noted that other seasons conflicted with their sport more than the hunters did—about twice as many times, in fact. I think this fits in with the overall dedication of the hunters to their sport when compared with the dropouts, many of whom probably participated in a number of autumn sports, while the hunters were more inclined to be waterfowl specialists.

Another area of complaint, "Behavior of other waterfowl hunters," was cited more by the hunters than the dropouts. We can assume that we're talking here about sky shooting and other unsportsmanlike activities that have a tendency to tighten the jaw of the active hunter. Table 19 backs up this complaint because the last category, "Hunter behaviors/sky shooting," shows that the dropouts were less concerned with this than were the hunters. Going back, we can see that more active waterfowlers were users of blinds and fewer were pass and jump shooters. Could it be that the complaints from the blind-loving active hunters about "hunter behavior" were really complaints about those who dropped out? In effect, are we seeing a thinning of the waterfowl ranks among those who are not "good" waterfowl hunters anyway? Let's take a look.

Table 20A shows that among those people who do their hunting in counties requiring steel shot, 14.2 percent of the dropouts, but only 10.7 percent of the *hunters*, felt that steel shot was unnecessary. As waterfowlers, we know steel shot is a fact of life in many areas, and we've got to learn to live with it because ducks can't live with lead.

The active waterfowler, where steel is required, recognizes this: a point in his favor. Okay, maybe steel isn't perfect, but who ever said that lead shot at 65 yards is perfect either, and every day in the marsh you'll see somebody try a 65-yard pull at a duck.

The hunter's attitude toward steel shot is part and parcel of his overall profile, I think, when compared with those who give up the sport. Again, let's take a look, based on this study, and draw a profile of the "average" waterfowler.

First, he's fairly well-educated, with some college in his bacground; more educated than the dropout. He makes more money, is slightly older, and got started in the waterfowling sports at an earlier age than his dropout counterpart.

He is dedicated to his sport, as shown by the fact that he hunts more days per season, is less influenced by other seasons that conflict with waterfowl seasons, and he is more likely to hunt well into the season, even when the weather turns nasty.

The average waterfowler complains less about the associated costs of waterfowling, recognizing the need for stamps and federal/state revenues for duck and goose management and habitat, and is more likely to understand and approve of steel shot if his hunting area requires its use.

He hunts more—mostly, in fact—from a blind, which brands him a better *technician* of the sport than his dropout counterpart who did a large amount of jump shooting and pass shooting— fine sports, mind you, but less likely to consistently produce good bags of ducks and geese.

He probably has more and better equipment because he has more money, has been at it longer, and his hunting methods are of the type that require equipment.

He is also more of a specialist than the dropout, going after a certain species in a prescribed manner rather than taking whatever happens to flap by.

He is also less tolerant of activities of other hunters that he sees as unsportsmanlike or detrimental to his enjoyment of the sport.

The dropout, on the other hand, appears to be marginally interested in the sport, and doesn't have the time, wherewithal or inclination to become a dedicated waterfowler. He may— may, mind you—be the person more often complained about by the other group, although I know of many cases where the dedicated hunter has been turned off by slob hunters and sky shooters and has packed in his waterfowling career.

So, even though the number of waterfowlers is declining across the United States, I think a shaking-down process is going on; the real hunters are sticking around, and those considered marginal are dropping out.

In the long run, I think this is good for the sport. By a process of attrition, we are sorting out the wheat from the chaff, and those left are more likely to be "good" hunters. This isn't to insult anyone; "good" doesn't mean "sportsmanlike" or "ethical." "Good," in this case, means knowledgeable and understanding of waterfowl and waterfowl management.

I was at the gun club the other day, had finished a couple rounds of skeet, and was laying waste to that facility's fine store of domestic distilled spirits, when the talk turned to waterfowling, as it often does.

A few of the lads were planning trips hither and yon in search of wildfowl shooting in the grand manner of yesteryear. A couple were going to Mexico, and several others were headed for the tundra. As we talked, some of the more experienced travelers drifted over and joined in, offering their advice.

The lure of Mexico could be summed up in the simple phrase, "lack of limits." That's not entirely true, of course, but what *is* true is that in many parts of the country the toll that can be legally taken on ducks and geese is staggering. The birds have funneled down the entire North American continent to spend the winter there, and "sportsmen" of the *Norteamericano* persuasion are, more and more, taking hunting trips there because of the liberal bag limits.

The word "liberal" is used under protest. I think that "hoggish" would be the better adjective here. And, under the guise of hunting, many of the gents from the States are carrying on a slaughter that would be unthinkable and illegal were it to be tried up north.

We have to remember that when the shooting on wintering fowl is great, it has an effect—a bad one—on the number of birds that return north to nest. Right now, the number of birds shot is small because the number of hunters is likewise tiny. But as time goes along, that's not likely to remain the condition.

Another problem facing the future of waterfowling is the tendency for sportsmen of the States to head into Canada for the ducks and geese that abound there. Again, there are heavy tolls taken per gun.

A good example of this is the way that some shooters are able to cut "deals" with the Indian guides around some goose camps. The Indians, by treaty, are guaranteed unlimited hunting for geese, which they will use for food during winter. Little problem here, except that with the welfare systems being what they are in the civilized world, I doubt if any Canadian Indians starve without 40 snow geese in the larder. But that's not the problem. The problem is that some Americans, knowing the treaty guarantees, will shoot as many geese as they can, giving the excess—over and above their own already liberal limits—to the Indians. Imagine shooting as many geese as you wanted, at an area where they are mainly young and naive under the guise that "nothing goes to waste."

Frankly, this stinks, and I've heard and read of shooters doing just this. This is being a pig, pure and simple. There oughta be a law.

I've read a lot from outdoor writers who decry the refuge system in this country, calling it artificial and saying that geese and ducks become, in effect, stupid freeloaders. Some of them also say that the refuges "shortstop" geese on their normal migration routes south, thus depriving hunters from shooting they used to get not too many years ago.

These people also note that they hate lining up for draws, and that they also hate all the regulations involved when hunting on publicly-owned areas.

Well, as the man once said, "tough."

The refuge system is the greatest thing to ever happen to waterfowl, waterfowl hunters and about 300 species of non-hunted wildlife. Period.

Without refuges, there would be wholesale diking, draining, filling, farming, developing and all the other things that conspired to make waterfowling such a tenuous sport before the refuges came along.

Okay, so maybe a refuge-reared goose in his first season isn't as smart as our paragons of sport would like, but I've read the work of these same people who just love hunting at James Bay or Hudson's Bay because of the fantastic shooting—shooting made fantastic because of a multitude of very young, very stupid geese.

Without the refuges, waterfowling, for many, would appear only in literature and limited edition prints.

End of sermon.

Obviously, there is only so much that any game department in any of the states is willing to do to bring the number of waterfowl hunters back into the fold. As the 21st century approaches, the steel-shot controversy still rages, especially among those who are not biologically informed. But the fact is that most informed, caring waterfowl hunters like the idea of steel shot because of its non-toxic nature, and they've learned to shoot it, handle the decreased ballistical efficiency, and regard it as a way to show that waterfowlers really do care about their sport—and the game they hunt.

As far as reducing the costs of fees and stamps, these monies are the main source for acquiring new wetlands at both the federal and state levels. Realistically, there's no way that these fees can be reduced or eliminated. As a waterfowl hunter, I'm glad that there are "non-paying" users enjoying the wetlands that my money helped buy and helps manage. I remind 'em of it every chance I get.

12

The Mistakes

The November day was but a promise as the Old Regulars pulled into the parking lot at the public hunting marsh. Before them, the world was a blanket of lifting fog, and the wind had started to freshen from the east. A hint of bad weather—a slight mist and a chill wind—could be felt under the fog, waiting.

There were four of them: Fred and Tom, who often hunted as a team, and Chuck and Mac, another pair. These four were not what you would be likely to call "World-Class Waterfowlers," but they enjoyed the sport. They just weren't real successful at it.

In the darkness, they unloaded the two canoes, the bags of decoys and Chuck's Lab. Guns, still cased, were placed in the canoes, and were joined by lunches, thermos bottles, metal am-

142

munition boxes and all the other condiments needed for a comfortable day in the blind. Chuck threw in a roll of chicken-wire fencing with cornstalks woven into it. This would be strung about his canoe to provide cover once they reached the area they would hunt.

Setting off in the darkness, the boys glanced at their watches and noted that they would have to hurry because shooting time was less than half an hour away. The motors sprung to life, sputtered, then caught, and they were off across the swamp. Around them, the sounds of the marsh were blocked by the engines, but they were aware that the place was starting to awaken. Once, Chuck saw a flight of ducks silhouetted against the eastern sky. The wind definitely had a bite in it.

Chuck and Mac stopped their canoe near a line of cattails that gave way to deeper water. They knew there were no other hunters about that area, and so they felt safe in setting up, knowing that they would not be disturbed. The line of cattails was long and unbroken, and so anyplace seemed okay to them. Fred and Tom motored deeper into the marsh.

Setting up, Mac hauled the decoys out into the area where he thought they would do the most to attract attention. He threw about a dozen to the left and another dozen to the right. The closest decoys were about 25 yards from the blind, the most distant about 60 yards. The decoys were well-scattered, giving the impression, Mac felt, of a contented group of dabblers at feed and rest along that line of cattails.

While Mac set the blocks, Chuck was busy rigging the cornstalk netting around the canoe. He was proud of that netting, and had used it with some success for several years. It was certainly easier to string the blind this way than to worry about cutting vegetation in the darkness. As he worked, he noticed flights of ducks overhead, birds that flared when they saw the two men moving below. It was going to be a fine day, yessir.

Meanwhile, Fred and Tom were choosing a place to set up. They decided that a stand of flooded timber offered little in the way of opportunity, so they instead chose an area of the marsh near the backwaters of the river that was the source of the flooding. Some beans had been planted and then covered over by water on the edge of this backwater—part of the cooperative sharecropping effort carried out by the game department and a local farmer.

This hunter has taken advantage of the natural vegetation to cover his blind. Many hunters try to make do with cover they bring along, and the results are easily detectable by waterfowl. Photo by Steven Griffin.

With an east wind in their faces, Fred and Tom arranged their decoys to give the impression of feeding birds—dabblers well-scattered and obviously concentrating on the food several inches below the surface. The cover was sparse in that area, so the boys had to move their hide back to an area where the game department had pushed some stumps into a pile. There, they sat atop the pushed-over wood and waited.

By now the morning flights had pretty well subsided, so Fred and Tom got out their lunches, poured some coffee, and ate. As with most waterfowlers, the time for lunch came about 9:30 in the morning.

Presently, a single bird came swinging in low behind them. They fumbled for their guns, but it was too late. They chuckled at their misfortune; when the same thing happened three more times, they used words they learned in the Army.

Meanwhile, back at the line of cattails, Chuck and Mac were doing no better. The birds that seemed interested in their spread initially swung by for one out-of-range look, and then continued on their way. Most of the flocks didn't even give the boys a second glance. By noon, they were discouraged.

By this time the wind had picked up and the birds were starting to move at both locations. Chuck and Mac noticed that the birds were funneling into an area of flooded woods, evidently to escape the wind and stinging sleet. They talked about moving, but decided that their setup was pretty good, and besides, why make all that effort when there were only a few hours of shooting time left?

Fred and Tom had moved off their perch atop the woodpile and were hunkered in their boat. They also saw the birds trading into the flooded woods, but decided to stay put as well. With darkness coming on, they were able to shoot one mallard that came in low on a pass over their decoys.

Then, just at the end of legal shooting time, a small flight of birds swung in toward their blocks. They stood and shot at the leaders, taking one of the birds. But, the rest flared and they got no follow-up chances. They were done for the day.

Picking up, they met Mac and Chuck on the way in. They had been skunked.

The fellows cursed their luck, the weather that had thoroughly wetted their hides, and the red fates, and headed for home.

Now, somewhere along the line, these men all made some costly mistakes. Like good golfers, the duck hunters who win are the ones who make the fewest mistakes over the long haul. Let's take a look.

First, Chuck and Mac set up their decoys along a long, unbroken line of emergent aquatic vegetation—the cattails. This line offered little in the way of harbors or small coves that would serve as natural gravitating spots for waterfowl. In other words, there was nothing about the location that would make it singularly appealing to waterfowl; hence, their decoys looked out of place.

Next, they made their site selection too late in the morning, as did Fred and Tom. The first birds were already moving while they were still setting out their blocks. Too late. They should have had things in order and in their hide long before legal shooting time.

Next, Chuck's cornstalk covering for the canoe was way out of place among the cattails. When in a certain vegetative type, you have to use that vegetation for cover.

Chuck and Mac's decoy setup was wrong as well. Given the east wind, it was apparent that bad weather was on the way. Yet, these lads set their blocks out to resemble an undisturbed flock of ducks, at ease on the water. The weather conditions should have put birds on the move, made them nervous. This should have been reflected in the decoy pattern. The decoys should have been bunched up—huddled—like dabblers are before a storm, when dropping air pressure puts them down onto the water. Coupled with the poor choice of location, their stool was definitely tacky.

Finally, when Mac was setting out the decoys, he placed them in a haphazard pattern, with the far ones out at 60 yards. This is poor placement and encourages bad range judgment on incoming birds. It also tends to make ducks decoy and swing well out.

For Fred and Tom, the decoy placement was a problem as well. In their flooded cropfield, the decoys may have looked natural, but they set up with the wind in their faces, which meant that any birds coming to the blocks would come in from behind them in order to land into the wind. This is just what happened several times. They also chose to sit up and watch the world—and the ducks—go by from atop a woodpile. This silhouetted them against the water and made them easier to see. Bad move.

When they noticed that the birds were using other areas, both pairs of hunters were reluctant to move. One of the primary lessons of waterfowling is that no set of decoys/blind/calling can be good enough to influence ducks away from an area that they want to use, and *to* an area they *don't* want to go. The lads should have been mobile enough to pick up and move.

Finally, when they did get a chance to shoot, Fred and Tom didn't handle the choosing of targets correctly. They took the front-end ducks first. What they should have done was wait until all the birds were in range, take their first shots at the tail-enders, and then mop up the closer birds last. Too bad—again.

All of this leads to a discussion of the most common mistakes made by waterfowlers. One of the first mistakes deals with the uncommonly good eyesight that ducks and geese possess. Like any creatures that have virtually inactive noses and hearing that isn't all that great, waterfowl have keen eyesight. First, waterfowl are not—make that NOT—color-blind. Witness the courting colors of mallards, if you need further proof. Those colors are there for other mallards to see, not you and me. So, any hint of an unnatural color is going to be picked up right off by a circling duck, the same as the color can be seen by humans.

The eyesight of waterfowl also tends to make the untidy litter around some blinds leap out as well. Empty, ejected shotshell hulls, lunch bags, a shiny watchband, the pretty blue wool gloves your Aunt Fishbait knitted for you. . . . all of these things present unnatural sights from above, and unnatural spells "danger."

Your bright, shining face may have won you your life's mate, got you your job, and made you an elder on the church board, but it scares hell out of ducks. Not long ago, I was doing some filming of a waterfowl hunting sequence for an outdoor television show. The plan called for us to do a scene in which we circled the decoys in a helicopter, much like the ducks would when decoying—sort of a duck's-eye view approach.

Below, the subjects in the blind were to try to look inconspicuous so that all would look natural from the air. The videotape was rolling, I was narrating into the cassette machine, and the chopper was humming. From below, one of the stars looked up at the aircraft. Immediately, his face leaped out like a mirror reflecting the sun.

We pointed this out on tape and continued. I took special notice of the Face Factor after that, and even when one of the guys would just peek up from under his hat brim, it showed. Camouflage clothing and meticulous blind building were both negated in one second by the glare from the face.

As experienced waterfowlers, we've all heard about this act of looking up. But until you've really seen it from the air, you can't imagine it. It just screams of humanity—and danger.

Movement—and lack of it—can be a factor as well. When people move, it shows. When a dog moves, it shows. These things were both observed from the air as well, and they were quite dramatic. It is imperative to stay still. As ducks approach, it's natural for us to sort of try to squinch our way into better shooting positions. But, even these slight movements are detectable from the air.

Lack of movement is something less-often analyzed. When the wind is really howling, everything moves—waves, decoys, cover—everything. When your blind is built of materials that do not allow for air movement, this shows too. I'd suggest that you use the native vegetation to at least reline your blind, if it is a permanent one, for each trip. This way, when the wind blows, the vagaries of the breeze will cause your part of the landscape to sway a little too, and you look less out of place.

Probably the single biggest factor accounting for unaccounted-for flare-offs has to be decoys. We've already talked about the openings that should appear, offering ducks a place to set down in shotgun range, so I'll not belabor that. When flaring takes place, it's pretty obvious to the gunners in the blind. The ducks head in, they take those last, few tentative and stabilizing wingbeats that serve to set them up for landing, and drop altitude. Suddenly the wings start beating again, there is a rapid gain in altitude and a change in direction—and they're gone.

Many times this is due to some movement, but it could just

This hunter has donned the greasepaint that takes the sheen from his face. An uncovered face and an unbowed head will send ducks and geese away like a neon sign. Photo by Steven Griffin.

be that there is something wrong in the decoys. It's always best to check them out if you're at a loss.

Check anchor lines. Sometimes the lines are too long and the decoys bob unnaturally. Other times the lines become tangled and wave action pulls some blocks below the surface. Tsk. Tsk. Still other times, the lines may be visible from the air, especially in super-clear water conditions. You may have to replace them with clear monofilament fishing line.

Ever had one lone decoy break off and drift away? This is a dead giveaway that something is amiss. It just doesn't happen like that in real life; ducks don't usually gang up and drum one of their number out of the Corps. Perhaps the setup is not in keeping with the weather; bad weather makes ducks nervous, and this should be reflected in the bunching of dabbler decoys. Too-serene an appearance can also alarm decoy-wise waterfowl, especially after they've been under the gun for several weeks.

Another common mistake is that of human nature, namely, the reluctance to stay out long enough to give your rig a chance. Some of my very best shooting seems to always come within a few minutes of the end of legal shooting time. Those last, precious flickers of daylight can be golden for the waterfowler, but too often we don't give them the chance to work their magic. I don't know how many times I've waited out a long and fruitless afternoon, thought about pulling up stakes early, and then stuck it out because I'm stubborn, only to be rewarded by a few grand moments of sport at the tag end of the day. Unlike other bird shooting sports, waterfowlers have to get used to the idea that their action will come in spurts. One minute of real adventure over a whole day can be considered exceptional in most parts of the country.

So, the lesson is to wait it out. At the end of the day, ducks are tired, usually hungry, they are less wary, they're looking for companionship and a chance to fill their bellies, and they are susceptible to the call and the decoys. Besides, the fading light tends to render their sharp eyes less effective, and they are more forgiving of your mistakes and movements. If I could hunt only 15 minutes at a time, it would be the last quarter-hour of the day, regardless of the weather.